The World's Stupidest

ATHLETES

BARB KARG
AND RICK SUTHERLAND

adamsmedia
avon, massachusetts

Published by
Adams Media, an F+W Publications Company
57 Littlefield Street, Avon, MA 02322
www.adamsmedia.com

The *World's Stupidest* Series published by special
arrangement with Michael O'Mara Books Ltd.

ISBN-10: 1-59869-572-X
ISBN-13: 978-1-59869-572-4

Printed in Canada.

J I H G F E D C B A

Library of Congress Cataloging-in-Publication Data
is available from the publisher.

This publication is designed to provide accurate and authoritative
information with regard to the subject matter covered. It is sold
with the understanding that the publisher is not engaged in
rendering legal, accounting, or other professional advice. If legal
advice or other expert assistance is required, the services of a
competent professional person should be sought.
—From a *Declaration of Principles* jointly adopted by a Committee of the
American Bar Association and a Committee of Publishers and Associations

Many of the designations used by manufacturers and sellers
to distinguish their product are claimed as trademarks. Where
those designations appear in this book and Adams Media was
aware of a trademark claim, the designations have been printed
with initial capital letters.

This book is available at quantity discounts for bulk purchases.
For information, please call 1-800-289-0963.

This book is dedicated to sports widows and widowers the world over; those patient souls who've been forced to sit through everything from midget Jell-o wrestling to twelve-hour quadruple overtime. We feel your pain.

And to all the moronic jocks who made this book possible with their incessant lying, cheating, doping, mouthing off, illicit debauchery, criminal acts, and major hissy fits.

Acknowledgments

Writing and producing a book is never an easy endeavor and *The World's Stupidest Athletes* is no exception to the rule. Thankfully, we're surrounded by a host of exceptional individuals who it is our privilege to know and to work with. For starters, we'd like to thank the fine folks at Adams Media with whom we've had the pleasure of working for many years. We offer our highest regards to director of innovation Paula Munier, the most brilliant gal we know, whose *joie de vivre* we appreciate and who we adore way more than cabernet and chocolate (and that's saying something!). We also salute Brendan O'Neill for his constant dedication, tenacity, and above all his sense of humor on each and every project. You guys are the best! As always, we also offer our sincere thanks to editorial director extraordinaire Laura Daly, copy chief Sheila Zwiebel, director of manufacturing Sue Beale, proofer Catherine Forrest Getzie, and designer Colleen Cunningham for their tireless and exceptional work. You guys are a fabulous team and we greatly appreciate everything you do.

On the homefront, we have the unending support of our families and friends, all of whom we would be lost without and who know that we've never *ever* done anything stupid. Uh huh. Our thanks to Ma, Pop, Dad, Chrissy, Glen, Anne, Terry, Kathy, the Blonde Bombshell, Ellen and Jim, Jeans and Jim, Jim V., Karla, Linda B., and the Scribe Tribe. You guys have all been a constant support and we consider your love and friendship one of the greatest gifts we could ever hope for. We love you all very much. We'd like to give a special shout to Chrissy Grant and Arjean Spaite, and as always to Trudi Karg and Ellen Weider for plowing through our endless humorous rantings and keeping us on the straight and narrow. To Chrissy, we'd like to offer additional accolades for her exceptional research, despite the fact that she's über-preggo! And last, but certainly not least, we thank our flurry of four-legged children, Piper, Jazz, Jinks, Maya, and Scout, who bring joy to our every waking moment. And our dear Sasha, Harley, and Mog who are always in our thoughts.

Many thanks to all of you!
Barb and Rick

Introduction

Athlete (a-th-leet)

A human possessing superior muscular function, natural talent, strategy, and staunch discipline that enable them to become superstars in various sports and heroes to millions of individuals worldwide.

Stupid Athlete (stoo-pid a-th-leet)

An über-muscular moron who displays superhuman feats of utter stupidity, bad sportsmanship, illegal activity, and who is dimwitted enough to hormonally warp their physique in order to beat the tar outta their opponents.

In the modern world, it's often hard to see how billions of individuals could possibly interact with each other given myriad cultures, religions, political attitudes, social, technical, and scientific aspects, cuisine, and everything in between. Fortunately, one of the few things that crosses all cultural barriers is sport, whether it's a Super Bowl, a curling match, a game of stickball, a marathon, a figure skating competition, or a simple round of hide-and-seek. All of the athletes who take part in sports become not only local heroes, but also national, international, and even worldwide icons. Some of the most popular individuals on the planet are athletes whether by virtue of their astonishing feats, the money they make, or the unbelievably moronic things they do.

Yes, it's true. Despite the fact that most athletes appear larger than life, when it comes right down to it they're capable of just as much stupidity as a buncha drunk rednecks going cowtipping after an all-night Budweiser bender. In many cases they're even more daft. Athletes are celebrities in all the countries of the world, and in smaller populations they're national heroes, which makes it all the more incomprehensible when they do something idiotic or violent, or simply exhibit bad sportsmanship. Watching an idol fall from grace is never pretty, no matter whether it's Kobe Bryant, Tonya Harding, Barry Bonds, Marion Jones, or coaches like Bobby Knight and Trevor Graham, or even commentators like that nasty nibbler Marv Alpert. And just like mere mortals, there are a few exceptional morons whose unforgivable acts just keep on giving, like the madness that is O.J. Simpson. The days of drug-free sport and good clean fun are dead and buried for the bleaters and cheaters who do their best to win at all costs. The bad apples disappoint us by shooting up performance enhancing drugs, playing the blame game when they fail to win, and wasting their God-given talents believing they're above the law. They are the quintessential *crème de la crème* of athletic stupidity and every time they pull a bonehead move we're there to watch them drown in their dolt-ish destiny.

In this snazzy little tome you'll find a full lineup of sports jocularity, quotes, bumper stickers, quizzes, awards, and a shameful tour de farce of various athletes who dug themselves a hole so deep that no quadruple axel, free throw, or last second Hail Mary could ever save them. In truth, no one ever hopes that an athlete of superior grace or talent, or even one who tries hard, will do something incredibly inane or disrespectful, but you can bet your gold-plated jockstrap that if one does falter before the finish line we're all gonna hit the replay more than once. That's a bet even Pete Rose would take. So pull up a bleacher seat, grab a plate of buffalo wings, and get ready to keep score of some major league athletic inanity, including:

Stupid Says . . . • Lamebrain athlete quotes

Bumper Snickers • Dimwit car decorations

Scatterbrained Sportsters • Can you say *duh*?

Football Faux Pas • Foolish footballers

Basketball Buffoons • Daft hoopsters

Baseball Boneheads • Birdbrain baseballers

Who's on First? • Bad coaches and managers

Food for Thought • Competitive eating world records

The Dumb Jock Dictionary • The "moronic athlete" meaning of words and phrases

Fan Foolishness • Sports fans gone wild

Nothing but Net • If athletes had Web sites

Oddball Athletics • Sports that no one should *ever* play

Jailbird Jocks • Athletes in trouble with the law

Running on Empty • Runners gone wrong

World Record Wackos • Bizarre athletic world records

Olympic Oops! • Bad Olympic behavior

The Ten Commandments of Stupid Athletes

I. Thou shalt not worship false deities save for John Madden, the Dallas Cowboy cheerleaders, and, above all, Keith Olbermann.

II. Thou shalt never take performance enhancing drugs unless otherwise directed by your coach who tells you that what you're taking is flaxseed oil or vitamin B-12 injections.

III. Thou shalt never under any circumstances give up beer, under-the-table kickbacks, fast cars, and even faster women.

IV. Thou shalt never murder your agent or adviser unless they're Mike Tyson or Marv Alpert, in which case be careful or you'll lose an ear and get nibbled to death while wearing trashy lingerie.

V. Thou shalt never give up the right to explain that your distinct lack of spelling, grammar, punctuation, and public speaking skill is a result of your dropping out of school after the third grade.

VI. Thou shalt never retain a mistress, stripper, or hooker, unless first having her sign legal papers saying she won't blackmail you, post your privates on MySpace, tell your wife, or sue you in excess of $100 million.

VII. Thou shalt never ever sell your jockstrap, ball cup, or used undies on eBay, or write some unintelligible crap autobiography snitching on your teammates and touting the virtues of drug-free sport.

VIII. Thou shalt watch your back when you're ahead, watch your front when you're behind, and when in doubt, thou shalt always punt.

IX. Thou shalt always maintain at any and all costs that your I.Q. is higher than an eggplant's.

X. Thou shalt not covet thy neighbor's trophies and season tickets even though you know he's a lying, cheating, no-good, backstabbing nincompoop and you deserve them more.

Food for Thought

Let it be said that competitive food eating is
a world entirely unto its own. Considered to
be athletes with a unique talent, top gurgitators are nothing less than astonishing and
incredibly baffling. You know that bloated
feeling you get after a huge Thanksgiving
meal? Remember that feeling when you picture competitive eater Patrick Bertoletti
scarfing down almost four pounds and thirteen ounces of roast turkey—in twelve minutes. Several pilgrims are turning in their
graves as we speak.

Oddball Athletics

Rugby is a tough enough game on the
ground, but underwater? Created by hardcore skin divers, underwater rugby is played
with a heavy sinking ball by teams of goggle-
wearing combatants in the deep end of the
pool. According to the rule book, drowning
your opponent is frowned upon.

Stupid Says . . .

66The word 'genius' isn't applicable in football. A genius is a guy like Norman Einstein.99

—Joe Theismann

Bumper Snickers!

I DIDN'T SELL MY SOUL TO SATAN.
IT'S A RENT-TO-OWN DEAL.
Michael Vick

SO YOU'RE A FEMINIST?
ISN'T THAT CUTE!
Bobby Riggs

Football Faux Pas

LeRon Landry, rookie for the Washington Redskins, was unable to practice at the start of their 2007 mini-camp due to a groin injury he sustained from a paintball accident. As a team-building exercise, coach Joe Gibbs let the players out of voluntary spring training early one day and many team members decided to blow some steam playing paintball. It was during that game that Landry took a shot to the groin. Teammate Marcus Washington said: "I didn't know paintball was that dangerous." Duh! Although Landry was expected to recover after a few days rest, FOX Sports reported that after a few minutes of watching practice on the sidelines Landry "left and began laboring slowly up the hill toward the team's main building, appearing to favor his left leg." Perhaps next time Landry will opt for a brush and not a gun when faced with a gallon of Dutch Boy.

The Doping Scandal of the Decade Award

The fact that athletes have been using steroids for decades is no secret, but it wasn't until 2003 that the practice of performance enhancement became a firestorm of illicit controversy triggered by a single word: BALCO. The scandal erupted when an anonymous tipster, later identified as track coach Trevor Graham, made a phone call to the United States Attorney in California about an undetectable steroid manufactured by the Bay Area Laboratory Co-Operative owned by Victor Conte, who along with V.P. James Valente, trainer Greg Anderson, and coach Remi Korchemny were surreptitiously distributing the drug to internationally renowned, world-class athletes. That phone call was followed by a package containing at least one used syringe that held traces of a designer steroid called tetrahydrogestrinone, also known as THG and more infamously as "the Clear." The Olympic Analytical Laboratory in Los Angeles quickly developed a process for detecting the banned substance and found that previously cleared samples from at least twenty athletes were tainted. On September 3, 2003, authorities raided the BALCO facilities and discovered a treasure trove of steroids, hoards of cash, and

more important, long lists of clients that
included some of the biggest names in sports.

All hell broke loose with the discovery that
Major League Baseball players such as Barry
Bonds, Jason Giambi, and Jason Grimsley
were on the client list, along with pro football
players Bill Romanowski and Chris Cooper,
and major track stars including sprinters Tim
Montgomery and Marion Jones. The steroid
shocker triggered accusations, denials, and
recriminations from the dozens of major players implicated in the scheme, followed by bans
and suspensions from athletic organizations
and criminal indictments that resulted in
BALCO's Conte and Anderson plea bargaining
their way into respective four- and thirteen-
month prison sentences for illegal steroid distribution and money laundering. Hardest hit
in the scandal were a dozen track greats who
would face permanent disgrace and financial
ruin, and ironically, Trevor Graham—the man
who kick-started the investigation and was
indicted for his shaky denial of involvement in
steroid distribution to his own athletes. The
BALCO fiasco exposed a cancer of unsports-
manlike hypocrisies in professional athletics
that makes stupidity look like an attribute.
And the repercussions are still reverberating
in every sport in the land.

Baseball Boneheads

In 1979, Rick Sutcliffe was the National League Rookie of the Year and pitcher for the Los Angeles Dodgers, but he and manager Tommy Lasorda had a rocky relationship. By 1981, Sutcliffe claimed Lasorda promised him a starting position, but instead, Lasorda omitted Sutcliffe from the postseason roster. What ensued was a tirade of epic proportion, with Sutcliffe bursting into Lasorda's office, smashing chairs, and overturning his desk. Sutcliffe later said in a 1986 interview with the Cub's team magazine: "He said to me 'you're lucky to be in the big leagues. You can't pitch in the big leagues.' That's when I picked him up by his uniform collar. I wasn't exactly choking him, but I guess my hands were sort of around his neck and I held him in the air and said: 'If you weren't fifty years old, I'd kick your ass.'" Not surprisingly, Sutcliffe was traded to the Cleveland Indians shortly thereafter.

Nothing but Net!

Monica Seles:
www.gruntersanonymous.org

Nancy Kerrigan:
www.whymewhyme.com

Don King:
www.whatsupwithmyhair.com

The Dumb Jock Dictionary

Sports terms and what dimwit sportsers think they are!

Umpire: *A tall building in New York*

Hat trick: *Something magicians do with bunnies*

Nordic combined: *A ménage à trois*

Bumper Snickers!

FREE EAR PIERCING!
Mike Tyson

HONK IF YOU WANT YOUR KNEECAP
SMASHED!
Tonya Harding

Running on Empty

New Yorker and marathoner Fred Lorz
thought he had the right stuff when he
started the marathon at the 1904 St. Louis
Olympics *and* when he crossed the finish line
first in three hours and thirteen minutes. But
Lorz wasn't as wiped out as his fellow competitors, probably because he gave up the
brutally hilly course after nine miles and
covered eleven miles by car. When his ruse
came to light, he claimed it was a practical
joke—but no one found it amusing, and he
was banned for life. (Curiously, the ban didn't
hold and Lorz went on to win the Boston
Marathon the following year.) What's truly
hysterical about that Olympic race were the
other competitors. The second place finisher
and eventual winner behind Lorz was Britain's Thomas Hicks, who had to be carried off
the track. Hicks was ready to give up ten
miles earlier but his entourage plied him with
brandy and doses of raw egg whites dosed
with strychnine sulfate. Cuban postman
Felix Carvajal lost all his money gambling en
route to the Games and had to run in his
street clothes. Unfortunately, he got hungry
during the race and stopped at an apple
orchard. After recovering from severe stomach cramps, Carvajal managed to cross the
line in fourth place!

Olympic Oops!

As one of the marquee sports of the Olympic
Games, it should come as no surprise that
more than a few swimming divas have taken
the plunge into bad sportsmanship. One of
those monstrous mermaids is American
swimmer and 1996 gold medalist Amy Van
Dyken, who at the 2000 Sydney Games
showed true American crass during the
semifinals of the women's 50-meter freestyle,
which placed her against Dutch aquawonder
Inge de Bruijn. Seething over de Bruijn's
gold medal and world record performances
in the 100 butterfly and 100 freestyle, Van
Dyken revved up and spit into de Bruijn's
lane. Unfazed, the Dutch dynamo obliter-
ated the world record, and left the audacious
Yank sputtering in her waves. Van Dyken,
hardly gracious in her defeat, left the pool
infamously stating: "If I were a man, I could
swim that fast," a statement that amounted
to accusations of drug use. During the finals,
de Bruijn again wiped the floor with her
rival and added a third gold medal to her
collection by swimming the second fastest
time in history. One hopes that all these
years later, Van Dyken has finally recovered
from her vapid brain chlorination.

The Scoreboard

The top ten sports movie sequels that never made it:

1. *Caddysmack*
2. *Million Dollar Rabies*
3. *Field of Screams*
4. *Seabisquik*
5. *The Bad News Bares*
6. *Raging Bullcrap*
7. *The Karate Squid*
8. *White Men Can't Plump*
9. *The Mighty Geese*
10. *Days of Dunderheads*

The Dumb Jock Dictionary

Sports terms and what dimwit sportsers think they are!

Bobsleigh: *A convicted murderer*

Pole vault: *Where strippers are interred*

Parallel bars: *Nightclubbing*

Oddball Athletics

For more than twenty-five years an odd competition between man and equine has kept
European athletes coming to Wales for the
annual Man Versus Horse race which pits
runners against mounted riders on a twenty-
two-mile course through the country's
roughest terrain. In 2004, a British Marine
made history by being the first human to
win the race, beating out 500 other runners
and more than forty riders. Okay Trigger,
who's your daddy now?

Basketball Buffoons

During his career, Wilt Chamberlain played for the Warriors, 76ers, Lakers, and even the Harlem Globetrotters. Known as "Wilt the Stilt" and "The Big Dipper," the seven-foot-one giant was a dominant force from 1959 to 1973, which earned him entry into the Basketball Hall of Fame and being named one of the fifty greatest players in NBA history. His antics off the court left a very different legacy. In his 1991 autobiography *A View from Above*, he made the outrageous claim that he'd slept with 20,000 women, an assertion that, if true, would've meant that he'd had sex more than nine times a week for forty years. (And this was before Viagra.) After the revelation, the "Stilt" became the butt of endless jokes and was criticized for his promiscuity by legendary tennis ace Arthur Ashe, who at the time was diagnosed with AIDS. Months later, fellow Laker Magic Johnson announced he'd contracted AIDS as a result of unprotected sex. Chamberlain eventually became an advocate for safe sex, saying that he should've explained the sexual climate of the era. Chamberlain died of heart failure in 1999 at age sixty-three. The final results of his sexual scorecard remain unknown.

Scatterbrained Grapplers

Match the wacky wrestler with his famous
finishing move:

1. Eddie Guerrero
2. Triple H
3. Chris Jericho
4. Hulk Hogan
5. Steve Austin
6. Chris Benoit
7. Mankind
8. Undertaker
9. Shawn Michaels
10. Ric Flair

a. Figure Four
   Leglock
b. Mr. Socko
c. Tombstone Pile
   Driver
d. Stone Cold
   Stunner
e. Crippler Crossface
f. Sweet Chin Music
g. Frog Splash
h. Atomic Leg Drop
i. Pedigree
j. Liontamer

Answers: 1-g,
2-i, 3-j, 4-h,
5-d, 6-e, 7-b,
8-c, 9-f, 10-a

26

Food for Thought

Under the heading of "no friggin' way in the universe," let's examine the world of condiments, namely mayonnaise and butter. In a feat that would cause immediate artery solidification in the diet conscious, Donald Lerman set a world record by eating seven quarter-pound sticks of salted butter in a mere five minutes. How yummy is that? And if that doesn't start your tummy gurgling, picture if you will, Ukranian Oleg Zhornitskiy who is the "Undisputed World Mayonnaise Eating Champion." At a mere 165 pounds, it took the thirty-six-year-old Zhornitskiy a paltry eight minutes to consume four thirty-two-ounce bowls of mayo. There's a Miracle Whip joke in there somewhere. . . .

The Dumb Jock Dictionary

Sports terms and what dimwit sportsers think they are!

Spikes: *Hypodermic needles used by steroid junkies.*

Pit crew: *A buncha broads who don't shave*

Giant slalom: *A tall rabbi*

Scatterbrained Sportsters

When Queensland rugby player Ben Czislowski unintentionally clashed heads with
Matt Austin during a Queensland Cup game
on April 1, 2007, both players were injured.
Czislowski need stitches and Austin broke
his jaw. No big deal for rugby, right? Guess
again. After the collision, Czislowski suf-
fered from lethargy, shooting head pain, and
an eye infection. Fifteen weeks later, he
finally went to his doctor and was shocked
to learn his symptoms were as a result of
Austin's infected tooth, which during their
collision was embedded into Czislowski's
forehead near his left eye. Czislowski said he
realized Austin lost some teeth, but assumed
they were on the ground. Now back to fighting form, Czislowski has Austin's tooth
proudly displayed on his bedside table, stating that if Austin would like it returned he'd
be happy to comply. But for now, Czislowski's
keeping it as proof the bizarre incident actually occurred. "It's a story I can tell for the
rest of my life. It will get a bit more exagger-
ated over the years, but it's a good laugh."
Kinda gives new meaning to the old adage:
"Give blood. Play rugby."

World Record Wackos

Every now and again you see those crazy karate guys who attempt to break two-by-fours with their head or punch through stacks of bricks, and it makes your head ache just watching it. In 2006, in Oslo, Norway, the Norwegian population was able to watch and ache as their fellow countryman Narve Læret went on live television and smashed ninety concrete blocks with one hand in sixty seconds. We're guessing that since that glorious achievement Læret has consumed no less than 2,800 cases of Advil. Give or take. . . .

Stupid Says . . .

❝I owe a lot to my parents, especially my mother and father.❞
—Olympic gymnast Paul Hamm

Oddball Athletics

Mixing brains with brawling, the European sport of chess boxing has taken the world by . . . uh . . . bewilderment. Here's the deal: Two competitors face each other in eleven alternating rounds: six rounds of chess lasting four minutes each, and five rounds of boxing that last two minutes each. You win by knockout, checkmate, or the referee's decision. Alrighty then. What's next? Scrabble wrestling?

Jailbird Jocks

Don King, legendary fight promoter and poster boy for really scary haircuts, has had numerous run-ins with the legal system. Over the years, he's been investigated by the FBI and even questioned by the U.S. Senate for alleged connections with Mafia don John Gotti, during which King relied on the protection of the Fifth Amendment. In the mid 1980s, the frighteningly coifed icon was indicted and subsequently acquitted of insurance fraud charges. King's most serious brush with the law came about in 1966 when he tracked down a man who owed him money and beat him to death on the streets of Cleveland, Ohio. Although he was convicted of second-degree murder, the judge in the case reduced the conviction to manslaughter, for which King served less than four years in the big house. Apparently, he finally learned his lesson, instead making a fortune out of arranging for other people to legally beat the crap out of each other in the boxing ring. And you wonder where Mike Tyson got his inspiration?

Olympics Oops!

Some athletes want an Olympic medal so bad they'll do anything to get it. A highly revered modern pentathlete, Ukrainian army officer Boris Onischenko won a silver medal in the 1972 Munich Olympics. Coming into the 1976 Montreal Games he again entered the penthathlon, a sport in which individuals compete in five events—swimming, shooting, horseback riding, cross-country running, and fencing. It was the latter that got him into big trouble. In fencing, a competitor scores a point when his sword, or épée, registers a legal hit on an opponent. Onischenko did a bit of revamping to his weapon, rewiring it so he could use his hand-to-trigger at will and register a hit on the electronic scoring system. British pentathletes became suspicious and raised the alarm. After winning one bout, Onischenko's next opponent, Britain's Jim Fox, protested that he was being scored against without the épée actually touching him. Officials finally gave Onischenko a different sword, and after analyzing his grip, which disguised his cheating mechanism, "Dis-Onischenko" was immediately disqualified. It must be said that in this instance, the hand was *not* mightier than the sword.

WHY DO PRO
BASKETBALL
PLAYERS DRIVE
B M W S ?

BECAUSE THEY
CAN SPELL IT.

The Worst Knock Knock Joke—Ever

The 1994 Lillehammer Olympics was one of the most sensationalized productions in Olympic history, but not for its showcase of athleticism. Sadly, it will be remembered for a pair of icy ballerinas whose tawdry soap opera makes Susan Lucci look like an amateur. It was the events prior to the Games, however, that sparked worldwide attention and left the names Tonya Harding and Nancy Kerrigan indelibly marked on history books—and not in a good way. The show of incredibly bad decorum, say nothing of horrid sportsmanship, took place at the U.S. World Championships after a practice session. As Kerrigan left the ice, she was suddenly whacked across the right knee with a metal baton. The image of her screaming "Why, why why?" will live in sports infamy. Harding suspiciously went on to win the title. Soon after, it was revealed that the assault was masterminded by Harding's ex-husband Jeff Gillooly and friend Shawn Eckhardt, and carried out by hired hand Shane Stant. Harding knew about it and helped cover it up—a move that utterly demolished her post-Olympic skating career.

Could They Be Any Dumber?

Match the moronic athlete with their bad behavior.

a. Mary Decker Slaney
b. Darryl Strawberry
c. Tonya Harding
d. Marty McSorley

e. Dennis Rodman
f. Pete Rose
g. Jennifer Capriati
h. Mike Tyson

1. Created a sex tape showcasing wedding night antics.
2. Ex-con who served time for tax evasion.
3. At age twelve was arrested in Brooklyn for purse snatching.
4. Olympic gold medalist who went through rehab after being busted for possession of marijuana.
5. Has been sued three times for alleged sexual battery and assaults on women.
6. Whined relentlessly after being accidentally tripped by Zola Budd.
7. Was suspended after beating a competitor with a stick.
8. Busted for cocaine and soliciting an undercover cop for hanky panky.

Answers:
1-c, 2-f, 3-h,
4-g, 5-e, 6-a,
7-d, 8-b

Nothing but Net!

Mike Tyson:
www.auralsurgery.org

Marion Jones:
www.ikilledmycareer.com

John McEnroe:
www.tempertantrums.com

Oddball Athletics

Imagine purposely throwing yourself into a dirty, stinky sixty-meter trench filled with water, muck, and peat moss. Clad in a wetsuit, goggles, and covered with forty pounds of sticky glop all you need to do is crawl 120 meters. Okey dokey. If you actually have the cojones for such an experience you'd be an official bog snorkler, and you'd probably be in Wales at the annual Bog Snorkling Championships. One word of advice: Don't forget to keep your mouth shut.

Bumper Snickers!

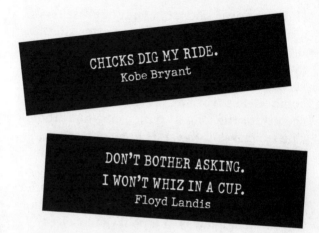

CHICKS DIG MY RIDE.
Kobe Bryant

DON'T BOTHER ASKING.
I WON'T WHIZ IN A CUP.
Floyd Landis

Acid Reflux of the Decade Award

If you're an entomologist read no further, because the sheer atrocity of this eating world record will likely give you a stroke. In 2001, a competitive eater by the name of Ken Edwards of Derbyshire, England, took it upon himself to rid the world of a few unpopular creepy-crawlies by eating thirty-six rather large Madagascar cockroaches in one minute. Yep. Sixty seconds. And the cockroaches were hissing. And you thought *your* indigestion was bad!

World Record Wackos

Have you ever taken out your aggression on a punching bag? If so, you can attest to the fact that after a few minutes, your shoulders are begging for death and your body is screaming for oxygen. That said, it should come as no surprise that there exists a world record for the longest punch-bag marathon. The surprise, however, is how long some bloke stood there punishing his body. In a two-day stretch in 2004, from June 15 to 17, American Ron Sarchian hung out at Premier Fitness in Encino, California. How long did Sarchian slug away at a poor defenseless punching bag? An astonishing thirty-six hours and three minutes. Makes you wonder how many people actually sat there and watched the ordeal. Seriously, how bored do you have to be?

Food for Thought

For most of us, a single slice of pie is plenty. Not so for competitive eaters. Theirs is a practice akin to one of the seven deadly sins. Case in point, Eric Booker, who at 420 pounds holds multiple world records. In 2004, Booker demolished almost five Entenmann's pumpkin pies in twelve minutes. Then there's Patrick Bertoletti, who in several 2007 competitions put down just over eleven pounds of Shoo-Fly Pies in eight minutes, more than fifteen pounds of strawberry shortcake in eight minutes, and just over nine pounds of blueberry pie in eight minutes—without using his hands. In 2006, he managed almost eight pounds of strawberry rhubarb pie in eight minutes, and almost eleven pounds of key lime pie also in eight minutes. Seems he's got a thing for eight-minute pie consumption. Not to be outdone, powerhouse eater Sonya Thomas demolished forty-six mince pies in ten minutes at a 2006 English competition, and in 2003, she did the unthinkable—she wolfed down almost five pounds of Wegman's Fruitcake in ten minutes. No doubt that's still residing in her colon as we speak.

Fan Foolishness

One of the wackiest traditions in hockey history has been carried on by fans of the Detroit Red Wings for more than fifty years. In 1952, fish shop owner and rabid Red Wings supporter Pete Cusimano tossed an octopus onto the ice at the start of a game leading into the Stanley Cup run. Each of its eight legs were meant to represent one of the games needed to win the Cup at that time. Oddly inspired, the Red Wings went on to sweep the series and a tradition was born. Bizarre as it may seem, octopi have been chucked onto the rink ever since. The NHL tried unsuccessfully to discourage the practice, but fans have taken to boiling the octopi to reduce the smell and smuggling them past security guards beneath bulky jackets. Al Sabotka, the building operations manager and Zamboni driver for the Red Wings has been happily cleaning up the splattered remains for nearly thirty years. According to Sabotka, an average of twenty-five octopi hit the ice during playoff games. In one game in 1995, a record was set when fans heaved fifty-four of the suckers over the railings!

Who's on First?

To a pro athlete, especially a finely honed runner, the most crucial element of their survival is their coach. For a handful of elite athletes, that coach was Trevor Graham and depending on how you analyze him, the guy is a modern-day Beelzebub. Former world record holder Justin Gatlin is just the last of at least six athletes who developed their skills under Graham's wing and were subsequently proven to have tested positive for illegal performance enhancing drugs. Graham is the guy who blew the whistle on the BALCO drug scandal, but that so-called altruism blew up in his face when suspicions were directed at his own distribution of steroids to his athletes. Too many top-ranked athletes who trained under him have been slapped with drug sanctions, including the recently disgraced Marion Jones, her former boyfriend and star sprinter, Tim Montgomery, former shot-putter C.J. Hunter, Antonio Pettigrew, Michelle Collins, Duane Ross, and Jerome Young, and it's likely they're going to talk about it in court. Life is not good for Graham, who's facing federal charges for perjury concerning his denial of steroid involvement, and it's probably going to get a lot worse.

Stupid Says . . .

"Listening to a woman is almost as bad as losing to one. There are only three things that women are better at than men: cleaning, cooking, and having sex.**"**
—Charles Barkley

The Dumb Jock Dictionary

Sports terms and what dimwit sportsers think they are!

Doubleheader: *What filthy rich baseball players hope for when hitting on a pair of busty groupies*

Super Bowl: *The* crème de la crème *of toilets*

Rookie: *A big hairy character in* Star Wars

Football Faux Pas

Warning: Perv alert! During a 2003 live broadcast of an ESPN interview, Hall of Fame quarterback Joe Namath had a close encounter of the lecherous kind. Suzy Kolber, ESPN's sideline reporter, was covering a Jets game and interviewed Broadway Joe. But Namath had apparently tipped the bottle one time too many prior to the airing, and when Kolber asked him what the team's struggle meant to him, he leaned in and said: "I want to kiss you." Kolber quickly wrapped up the interview and replied: "Thanks Joe. A huge compliment." But did that stop the renowned gridster? Nope. Namath repeated his request one more time before Kolber turned the broadcast back to the announcers. The randy footballer later apologized and—get this—admitted to a problem with alcohol. *Ya think?* Namath entered an alcohol treatment program in 2004, but it remains unclear if he conquered his penchant for drunken puckering.

Jailbird Jocks

The biggest scandal to rock the sports world in 2007 was the horrific revelation that Atlanta Falcons quarterback Michael Vick was the financial genius at the top end of an illegal dog fighting operation known as "Bad Newz Kennels," which operated on Vick's rural Virginia property. Although Vick initially proclaimed innocence and wounded indignation at such appalling accusations, state and federal prosecutors gathered damning evidence and leaned on coconspirators hard enough that they ultimately turned on Vick to reduce their own prison sentences. What made the matter so ugly was that there was overwhelming evidence that Vick himself participated in executing both wounded and nonaggressive dogs who wouldn't fight. Thankfully, the scandal destroyed Vick's lucrative football career, his estimated $26 million annual salary and endorsements dwindling to zero, and got him a one-way trip to the slammer for twenty-three months.

WHAT HAS FOUR LEGS AND NO EARS?

MIKE TYSON'S PET CAT.

What's in a Name?

The top ten Major League Baseball teams that never made it.

1. Los Angeles Codgers
2. Seattle Marinaters
3. Chicago Pink Socks
4. Baltimore Oreos
5. New York Hanky Pankys
6. Kansas City Boils
7. Minnesota Triplets
8. Philadelphia Sillies
9. Detroit Blighters
10. Florida Martians

Oddball Athletics

One of the oldest annual extreme sports events in England has been going on for centuries, with some historians claiming it dates back to pre-Roman times. This legendary U.K. sport is "cheese rolling," and every year hundreds of hardy souls race in heats down a steep and treacherous hill chasing after an eight-pound wheel of ripened cheese. No joke. Some win, some lose, and a lot of crazy folks get hurt in the frenetic free-for-all, which attracts thousands of screaming fans. No doubt Gouda fun is had by all.

Baseball Boneheads

Wade Boggs is a baseball Hall of Famer and former third baseman who spent the majority of his career with the Boston Red Sox. But his image was severely tarnished in 1988 when the married Boggs admitted to a long extramarital affair with Margo Adams, who filed a multi-million-dollar lawsuit against him claiming he reneged on his promise to pay her for wages she lost while traveling with him for four years. In 1989, Adams posed for *Penthouse* and gave an interview detailing their affair, while also disclosing negative remarks that Boggs made about fellow teammates. In his defense, the adulterer told Barbara Walters in an interview that Adams threatened to make his life difficult if he ended the relationship. He also feared she would blackmail him. Later that year, Adams and Boggs settled out of court for an undisclosed amount. Ain't love grand?

Basketball Buffoons

Los Angeles Lakers superputz Kobe Bryant found himself in a world of hurt in 2003 when Katelyn Faber accused him of raping her in a Colorado hotel room. The accusation triggered a messy media frenzy that made Bryant a national and tabloid headliner for months, and caused the cancellation of endorsement contracts with industry heavy-weights McDonald's and Nutella. Faber faced her own publicity demons with virulent reactions from Bryant fans, and although media outlets traditionally refuse to divulge the names of alleged rape victims, Faber's name, address, and phone number quickly surfaced on the Internet. Multiple death threats against her ended with FBI investigations and the imprisonment of two men in unrelated incidents of criminal conduct. A criminal trial against Bryant was dropped in 2004 after a reluctant Faber refused to testify. Instead, she filed a civil suit which was ultimately settled out of court for an undisclosed amount and included a vague public apology from Bryant. Whether the situation was truly a case of rape by Bryant or an attempt at earning a huge financial payoff by Faber will never be known.

Stupid Says . . .

❝I am beautiful, famous, and gorgeous.**❞**
—Anna Kournikova

Nothing but Net!

Kostas Kenteris:
www.awolurinalysis.org

Barry Bonds:
www.imafrigginmoron.com

Paul Hamm:
www.goldmedalwhiner.com

Food for Thought

Okay, so pretend for a moment you're a competitive eater. If you could choose anything that you could consume, what would you choose? Would it be dill pickles? Seriously. Why pickles? And why not sweet pickles? Apparently the pickle problem didn't bother Cookie Jarvis. He devoured almost three pounds of sour pickles in five minutes. Five minutes! That's a minute less than it took Brian Seiken to down more than two and a half pounds of vinegar pickles. Makes you pucker just thinking about it. . . .

Running on Empty

Stanislawa Walasiewicz, aka Stella Walsh, was born in Poland in 1911. A highly gifted sprinter, she competed on the international circuit and became not only the most popular Pole, but the most dominant sprinter of the 1930s and 1940s. At the 1932 Olympic Games she won the 100 meters and tied the world record, but at the 1936 Berlin Games she won silver, losing to American arch-rival Helen Stephens. In a controversial move, and at the rumored behest of Walsh supporters who claimed Stephens might be a man, Stephens was subjected to a humiliating medical inspection after which she was pronounced female. In 1947, Walsh married boxer Neil Olson and by 1975 she became a Hall of Famer. Sadly, she was shot in 1980 during an Ohio shopping center robbery, after which her mystique took a bizarre turn. During her autopsy it was discovered that Ms. Walsh wasn't a Ms. at all—she was a Mister! Suffering a form of mosaicism, she had chromosomes from both sexes. In Walsh's case, she also had male genitalia. For sixty-nine years, she kept her brilliant reputation intact from start to finish. Now *that* took some cojones!

Stupid Says . . .

"All hockey players are bilingual. They
know English and profanity.**"**

—Gordie Howe

The Dumb Jock Dictionary

Sports terms and what dimwit sportsers
think they are!

Astroturf: *What Neil Armstrong walked on*

First base: *Where one hopes to get on
a first date*

Draft pick: *Budweiser or Old Milwaukee*

World Record Wackos

You might not immediately know what a shuttlecock is, but if you've ever played badminton you'll recognize it as the plastic "birdie" you swat back and forth. A typical shuttlecock is comprised of feathers attached to a cork in a conical shape. That said, imagine trying to juggle a shuttlecock between your feet for a prolonged period of time much like a hacky sack. Sound difficult? It wasn't for Li Huifeng of China who in 2004 did just that—nonstop, without the shuttlecock touching the ground—for four hours and thirty-seven minutes. And you thought badminton was for sissies!

HOW MANY FOOTBALL PLAYERS DOES IT TAKE TO CHANGE A LIGHT BULB?

FOUR. ONE TO CHANGE THE BULB, AND THE OTHER THREE TO ARGUE WHETHER OR NOT IT'S OVER THE END ZONE.

Who's on First?

In 1978, Tommy Lasorda was the L.A. Dodgers manager when he unleashed a legendary obscenity-filled rant after Chicago Cub Dave Kingman hit three home runs during a regular season game to bring the Cubs to victory. After the game, reporter Paul Olden asked Lasorda what his thoughts were on Kingman's performance, after which Lasorda spewed his infamous tirade:

"What's my opinion of Kingman's performance!? What the BLEEP do you think is my opinion of it? I think it was BLEEPING BLEEP. Put that in, I don't BLEEP. Opinion of his performance!!? BLEEP, he beat us with three BLEEPING home runs! What the BLEEP do you mean 'What is my opinion of his performance?' How could you ask me a question like that, 'What is my opinion of his performance?' BLEEP, he hit three home runs! BLEEP. I'm BLEEPING pissed off to lose that BLEEPING game. And you ask me my opinion of his performance! BLEEP. That's a tough question to ask me isn't it? 'What is my opinion of his performance?'"

Fan Foolishness

North American sports fans are well known for their intense and often bizarre antics when it comes to supporting hometown teams. Fortunately, we don't hold a candle to Brazilian soccer fans, who have been known to start riots and fistfights with rival fans. In São Paolo, Brazil, fan rivalry became nearly—and literally—explosive in June 2007 when two Palmeiras soccer fans were arrested after following a bus loaded with opposing team supporters on their way back to their hometown of Cruzeiro. During a routine inspection at a highway checkpoint, Jefferson Lima and Jorje Sampaio were caught with a live hand grenade that they intended to toss into the bus in retaliation for a 3-1 loss at a São Paolo stadium. Makes Tyson seem like a pussycat, don't it?

The Dumb Jock Dictionary

Sports terms and what dimwit sportsers think they are!

Stats: *38-24-38*

Defense: *What you have in your backyard*

Luge: *What baseball players hock up and spit out before every pitch*

Bumper Snickers!

WHAT HAPPENED IN VEGAS SHOULDA
STAYED IN VEGAS.
O.J. Simpson

COULD I BE MORE GORGEOUS?
Anna Kournikova

Oddball Athletics

On Labor Day weekend in 1992, the first ever lawn mower race was held in Grayslake, Illinois, and since then the sport has spread like fertilizer across a nation filled with easily amused sports fanatics. As a matter of interest, modified lawn mowers used for racing can hit an astonishing eighty-five miles an hour on the straightaways and blaze around corners like sports cars. Finally! The perfect sport for couch potato NASCAR junkies. Hallelujah!

Olympic Oops!

There are few titles in the sports world more coveted than "the world's fastest man," and that was never more apparent than at the 1988 Seoul Olympics. It was the final of the 100 meters, and the race was destined for world record time with Britain's Linford Christie, Americans Calvin Smith, Dennis Mitchell, and Carl Lewis, and Lewis's arch rival, Canadian Ben Johnson. After the gun went off, the first man to cross the line was Johnson in a time of 9.79—the fastest time in history. Christie pulled up second, and a stunned Lewis came in third. But Johnson's victory was short lived. After the medal ceremony, his urine tested positive for the anabolic steroid Stanozol. His excuse was that he consumed a spiked herbal drink, but that didn't deter the IOC, who cast him out of the Games. He was then stripped of all his titles and awards and banned from competition for two years. In 1993, he again tested positive and was banned for life. From "world's fastest man" to "world's most disgraced man" in less than ten seconds. The irony is inescapable.

Mix and Mingle:
Asinine Athlete Anagrams

1. Floyd Landis
2. Anna Kournikova
3. Darryl Strawberry
4. Joe Theisman
5. Tonya Harding
6. David Beckham
7. Charles Barkely
8. Diego Maradona
9. Mike Tyson
10. Dennis Rodman

a. HYDRATION NAG
b. INNARDS DEMON
c. BACK MAD HIVED
d. AN AVIAN KOOKURN
e. FINALS ODDLY
f. MONEY SKIT
g. BASAL CHERRYELK
h. ENEMA HISJOT
i. DRYRASTRY BRAWLER
j. ANDROID OMEAGA

Answers: 1-e,
2-d, 3-i, 4-h,
5-a, 6-c, 7-g,
8-j, 9-f, 10-b

59

Scatterbrained Sportsters

No sports figure in history has achieved the notoriety of Michael Gerard Tyson for purely outlandish behavior. After being convicted of rape in February of 1992, Tyson spent three years in an Indiana prison, after which he went on a quest to win boxing titles that eventually put him in the ring against former heavyweight champ Evander Holyfield. Their first match in 1996 resulted in a contentious win by Holyfield, with Tyson's camp crying foul over alleged head-butting. The loss apparently made Tyson hungry for a rematch, which happened the following year. After three rounds of more alleged head-butting, Tyson chose the unusual retribution of biting off part of Holyfield's ear and spitting it onto the arena floor. The fight was immediately stopped, Holyfield was declared the winner, and the fight crowd rioted, injuring several spectators. Tyson went on to win and lose more highly controversial bouts until his retirement in 2005, but none would come close to the debacle of the ear chomping episode that made Iron Mike the most dangerous sports thug both in and out of the ring.

Stupid Says . . .

"When you say I committed adultery, are you stating before the marriage of 1996 or prior to?**"**

—Dallas Cowboys cornerback
Deion Sanders

Food for Thought

You know what they say about oysters? Well, lets hope in this case the aphrodisiac myth is false. On March 20, 2005, Sonya Thomas devoured forty-six dozen Acme Oysters at the New Orleans Acme Oyster House in a mere ten minutes. For the morbidly curious, Ms. Thomas, one of the world's top professional gurgitators, is in her early forties and weighs a whopping 105 pounds. Dieting is obviously *not* an issue.

Bumper Snickers!

I MAY BE A CHAUVINIST BASTARD.
BUT I'M DAMN GOOD AT IT.
Charles Barkley

HONK IF YOU'VE LIED
TO A GRAND JURY!
Barry Bonds

Stupid Says . . .

"He speaks English, Spanish, and he's bilingual too."

—Don King

Smarter Than the Average Bear?

When it comes to sheer hilarity in the sports world, there is arguably no one more quotable than Lawrence Peter "Yogi" Berra. A Hall of Fame catcher, record setter, and fifteen-time All-Star, Berra went on to become a successful and beloved Major League coach and manager. In short, he's one of the most renowned baseballers in history. His comments, however, are equally historic for a different reason.

66Predictions are difficult, especially about the future.99

66Baseball is 90 percent mental and the other half is physical.99

66In theory there is no difference between theory and practice. In practice there is.99

66I never said most of the things I said.99

66If people don't want to come out to the ball park, nobody's gonna stop 'em.99

66That ain't the way to spell my name.99
   —After he got a check that read "Pay to bearer"

Jailbird Jocks

Considering how many little boys dream of growing up to be pro footballers, too many of them manage to screw up their dream once they've accomplished it. Adam "Pacman" Jones is one of those dolts, having been arrested numerous times for a host of criminal offenses. In 2007, the star Tennessee Titan cornerback was suspended for the season after a spree of altercations in Las Vegas. On February 19, 2007, the pinhead got into a tussle in a Vegas strip club after joining rap singer Nelly in raining hundreds of one dollar bills onto a stage. When a dancer attempted to gather the loot, Jones snapped. He grabbed the poor woman by her hair and slammed her head onto the stage, which triggered a confrontation with a club security guard whom Jones threatened to kill. After leaving the club, one of Jones's entourage returned and started shooting, hitting the guard, another patron, and paralyzing former pro-wrestler Tommy Urbanski from the waist down. Faced with felony counts for conspiracy, Jones accepted a plea deal that will put him in the hoosegow for a year. Final score? Zero points for Pacman.

Baseball Boneheads

All-Star pitcher Kevin Brown signed a $105 million contract with the L.A. Dodgers after the 1998 season. In 1999, the rookie became flush with anger when, after a workout, he took a shower in the Dodgertown clubhouse. What caused the hissy fit? A teammate flushed a toilet which caused the shower to heat up, scalding the hot head. Enraged over the change in temperature, Brown proceeded to take a bat and beat the hell out of the offending toilet. In a pathetic attempt at damage control, Dodgers manager Davey Johnson said: "He did something I'd like to do many times when I was in the shower and someone flushed the toilet." But the anger didn't stop there. Following his 2006 retirement, Brown was accused by a neighbor of pulling a gun on him in a dispute over yard debris. The altercation allegedly began when the neighbor saw Brown throwing grass clippings into his yard. Presumably, the neighbor returned the favor, after which Brown confronted him. Both parties declined to file charges. A hundred million bucks and you can't afford a gardener? Pfft. . . .

Nothing but Net!

Floyd Landis:
www.testosterone.com

Justin Gatlin:
www.twostrikesyerout.com

Darryl Strawberry:
www.imaloser.com

The Dumb Jock Dictionary

Sports terms and what dimwit sportsers think they are!

Jersey: *The name of the state right next to New York*

Pitcher: *A pretty image, usually in a frame*

Bleachers: *Faux blondes*

Food for Thought

In the bizarre world of competitive eating, few foods have escaped being utterly and messily devoured, but when it comes to pork, it's Joey Chestnut who brings home the bacon. Currently ranked number one with the International Federation of Competitive Eating (IFOCE), and with over a dozen world records down his gullet, Chestnut is the guy to beat. In 2006, the eating machine set two of his records, the first at the Chinook Winds Casino in Lincoln City, Oregon, where he downed almost eight and a half pounds of pork rib meat in a blazing twelve minutes. Next up were pulled pork sandwiches, a mere ten minute performance that wiped forty-five sandwiches off the face of the planet. Two weeks later, on September 16, Chestnut visited the Horseshoe Casino Council Bluffs and confronted a pile of pulled pork. Amazingly, it took only ten minutes to scarf down just over nine and a half pounds of the smoked oinker. Considering Chestnut is only twenty-three, pigs the world over should be afraid. *Very afraid*.

Football Faux Pas

When Detroit Lions wide receiver Roy Williams announced in a radio interview that he's an über-cheapskate it brought about a wave of criticism considering his $1.5 million annual income. "I am cheap. I'm a cheap date," Williams boasted. "Get you some McDonald's, with some cheese on it, and I'm just really cheap, man." When asked about tipping the pizza delivery person, Williams asserted that "There's no such thing as a tip. But I'm really polite and I say, 'Thank you sir.' The pizza man knows, when he comes to my address, he's coming for free." After the interview, Pizza Hut president Scott Bergren challenged Williams to be a delivery driver for one day, in return for Pizza Hut forgiving his past tipping transgressions. In October of 2007, Williams agreed to deliver pizza and donate his tips plus $5,000 to the World Food Organization, with Pizza Hut matching his donation. But Williams quickly got a taste of his own medicine when his first two deliveries stiffed him. True to his word, Williams turned over a new leaf. The following week he tipped the pizza delivery person seven bucks. Nice going Ebenezer.

Fan Foolishness

In 2007, a Queens, New York, man became so upset that the Mets were losing that he actually stabbed and bludgeoned his sixty-one-year-old mother, Maria Fischman, to death with a twenty-pound barbell. Michael Anthony, twenty-six, became so enraged over the Mets 6-5 loss to the Washington Nationals that he began banging on the walls. His father, Fred, ordered him to stop, but Anthony punched him in the face and threw him to the ground. "We started fighting and my mother jumped in," Anthony told police, noting that she took a knife from the kitchen. After a struggle with her son ended with her being stabbed in the head, Fischman ran into the bedroom. Anthony, fearing she was retrieving a weapon from a dresser drawer, grabbed the barbell and took several swings. Fischman was struck several times and fell to the floor. Anthony was arraigned on murder, weapons, and assault charges, and ordered held without bail. With any luck, this dumbbell will serve the rest of his life in hoosegowjail with limited television privileges.

Bumper Snickers!

IF YOU'RE CUTE, I'M A LECH.
Joe Namath

WHAT WOULD CARTMAN DO?
Brian Boitano

World Record Wackos

Beach volleyball is always fun to watch,
what with all those gorgeous sweaty guys
and gals smacking at balls and kicking up
sand on some beautiful beach. Hardcore
fans are known to spend days watching
their favorites play week-long tournaments,
but it must've taken serious overzealous fans
to hunker down at Western Australia's Bun-
bury Indoor Beach Volleyball Centre in
November of 2005 to watch the world's longest single game of indoor beach volleyball.
How long did the game last? Believe it or not,
it went on for fifty-one hours. That's eleven
hours longer than an average work week.
And a lot more fun, come to think of it.

Stupid Says . . .

Sometimes, there's just nothing better than trash talk among rival boxers—especially the true legends:

66He's phony, using his blackness to get his way.99
— Joe Frazier on Muhammad Ali

66Joe Frazier is so ugly he should donate his face to the U.S. Bureau of Wildlife.99
— Muhammad Ali

Running on Empty

For anyone who closely follows track and field, the revelation that sprinter Marion Jones took steroids came as no surprise. Dogged for years by allegations and surrounded by busted enablers including ex-husband C.J. Hunter, ex-boyfriend and world record sprinter Tim Montgomery, and coach and BALCO mess Trevor Graham, Jones remained steadfast that she was clean. Liar! A positive test for EPO in 2006—which was cleared after a negative second sample—set the stage for her ultimate confession. On October 5, 2007, she finally admitted that during the 2000 Sydney Games, in which she was America's darling, she was under the influence of the designer steroid THG, which she claimed Graham told her was flaxseed oil. The IAAF annulled her records, stripped her of her medals, imposed a two-year ban, and ordered repayment of $700,000 in prize money. Jones's lying to Feds will likely garner jail time, with secondary charges pending for lying about Montgomery's fraud case. Excuses aside, there's nothing Jones can do to make restitution for the fact that she cheated. Call a spade a spade. She robbed fellow competitors of their moment of glory. Bad karma, lady. Bad karma. . . .

WHY DO FOOTBALL PLAYERS PREFER PLAYING ON ARTIFICIAL TURF?

IT STOPS THEM FROM GRAZING.

Olympic Oops!

Most of the retired male figure skaters we know about have gone on to careers in professional skating, coaching, and broadcasting, but one skater in particular took the unusual step of entering professional kidnapping. Wolfgang Schwartz, winner of the men's singles title at the 1968 Grenoble Olympics, was convicted of human trafficking after smuggling five women from Russia and Lithuania into Austria to work as prostitutes in 2002. For his efforts, Wolfie won eighteen months in the hoosegow. Then he upped the stupidity ante in 2006 when he was convicted of plotting the kidnapping of the daughter of a prominent Romanian businessman and holding her for a $4 million ransom. Inexplicably, the disgraced ice prince came right out and confessed, and it was back to the pokey to serve an eight-year sentence. We're guessing Wolfie's new cellmate, Bubba, will be more than happy to see his triple Salchows.

What's in a Name?

The top ten NFL teams that never made it.

1. Saint Louis Clams
2. Baltimore Mavens
3. Oakland Sadists
4. Cincinnati Bagels
5. New England Matriarchs
6. Indianapolis Dolts
7. Dallas Sowboys
8. Philadelphia Beagles
9. Cleveland Clowns
10. Green Bay Snackers

The Dumb Jock Dictionary

Sports terms and what dimwit sportsers think they are!

Fly ball: *Joining the mile high club*

Blitzed: *Babe Ruth's condition between games*

Bowl game: *Tossing Cheerios into the toilet for target practice*

World Record Wackos

There's no doubt that some individuals on the planet have a particular talent, but few can lay claim to the God-given ability of Michael Kettman. What makes this bloke so special, you ask? Well, on May 25, 1999, Kettman accomplished something that most of us couldn't execute if our lives depended on it. Hailing from St. Augustine, Florida, Kettman traveled to London, where he was able to spin twenty-eight basketballs all at the same time. Twenty-eight! If that didn't make the Harlem Globetrotters jealous, nothing will.

Bumper Snickers!

I DO WHATEVER MY
RICE KRISPIES TELL ME TO.
Dennis Rodman

I SWEAR I WAS JUST SELLING
VITAMINS.
Victor Conte

Stupid Says . . .

"We are going to turn this team around 360 degrees.**"**

—NBA player Jason Kidd

Scatterbrained Sportsters

Some morons will do anything to pass a drug test, but this idiot takes the cake. In 2007, Romanian weightlifter Victor Alexandru Pretoi was banned for two years after he tried to alter the results of his drug test by hiding his father's urine in a condom and attempting to use it as his own. Petroi's nervous behavior during an out-of-competition drug test raised a red flag, so testers searched him and uncovered his diabolical scheme. A spokesman from Romania's anti-drug agency, ANAD, explained that Pretoi, a weightlifter from the Steau club, was hiding the condom in his left palm. Worse yet, his manager was in full cahoots with the plot. What a dillweed! Holding it in his hand? Who shows up to a drug test with a urine-filled rubber in their hand?

Stupid Says . . .

❝I can't really remember the names of the clubs that we went to.❞
—Shaquille O'Neal when asked if during his stay in Greece he visited the Parthenon

Viral Athletes

Match the lamebrained sportster with their computer virus!

a. Marion Jones
b. Michael Vick
c. Tom Brady
d. Anna Kournikova
e. Nancy Kerrigan

f. Barry Bonds
g. John McEnroe
h. Mike Tyson
i. Dennis Rodman
j. O.J. Simpson

1. If you run a virus check you get a message telling you that you have so many viruses that you're beyond repair.
2. When you shut down your computer, it starts screaming "Why me? Why? Why?"
3. When you hit the escape key, you get a message asking you to pee in a cup.
4. If you hit the back slash, Fred Goldman shows up at your front door.
5. Every time you type in the word "steroid," the computer asks you why you lied to a grand jury.
6. When you Google "going to hell" it takes you to P.E.T.A.'s top ten most wanted list.
7. Every time you access the Victoria's Secret Web site you get a message telling you to dump Gisele Bündchen.
8. Whenever you access your MySpace page you get instant messages telling you that you're conceited.
9. When you boot up, your mouse bites you on the ear.
10. When you eject a DVD, your machine starts screaming that you're an incompetent clod.

Answers: 1-i,
2-e, 3-a, 4-j,
5-f, 6-b, 7-c,
8-d, 9-h, 10-g

Jailbird Jocks

Hiring a goon to murder your sports agent is never a good idea, but for Mike Danton, former left winger for the St. Louis Blues pro hockey team, hiring a police dispatcher to do the job was even worse. Two days after the Blues got knocked out of the 2004 Stanley Cup race, Danton was arrested for conspiracy to kill his agent, David Frost, and immediately confessed to the crime. For the dastardly deed, Danton was sentenced to seven-and-a-half years in a federal prison without parole, and will be extradited to his home country of Canada and denied return entry into the United States, which will effectively kill his hockey career for good. Although he didn't deserve death, it should be noted that David Frost is no angel either. Frost, who was Danton's junior league hockey coach before he turned pro, is accused of sex crimes against three girls and four boys all under the age of eighteen. Takes one thug to know another. Blech.

Basketball Buffoons

For a kid with a bright chance of making it into pro basketball, Kenny Brunner has gone out of his way to screw up. In March 1998, as a rising college star power forward and recruit for California State University, Fresno, Brunner was arrested along with teammate Avondre Jones for threatening an acquaintance in an altercation over a television program. Jones allegedly pulled a handgun, after which he and Brunner decided to use different weapons. Their weapons of choice? Samurai swords. On top of that, Jones stole a camera and $230 in cash from the poor victim. Although Jones was convicted and tossed off the team, Brunner managed to avoid trial due to insufficient evidence. But that didn't last long. Later that year, Brunner was arrested again for threatening to kill Los Angeles City College's basketball coach Mike Miller. He spent five months in lockup awaiting trial, and once again lucked out when charges were dropped. The kid's still looking for a college to play out his NCAA years, but hasn't found one that will take him on. No word on whether the NBA will risk taking him either.

The Unhappiest Guest on Earth Award

Like most disciplines, ice skating is a cut-throat sport where the stakes are high and there's big money to be made for gold medalists. The 1994 Lillehammer Olympics proved tumultuous for Nancy Kerrigan, having conquered the vicious Tonya Harding gang, but losing gold to Ukrainian Oksana Baiul. Normally, it's the gold medalist who wins the big endorsements, but in this instance it was Kerrigan's elegance and all-American charm that won people over. Yeah, *right*. After spouting off a few choice snarks at the judges and Baiul prior to the medal presentation, Kerrigan bagged on the closing ceremonies and departed for a publicity parade at Walt Disney World, which was sponsoring her for a cool $2 million. But while riding atop a fire engine with Mickey Mouse, a whinefest most unbecoming of an Olympic idol ensued: "This is dumb. I hate it. This is the most corniest thing I have ever done," said Kerrigan. Claiming her words were taken out of context, she alleged she was unhappy about having to wear her silver medal. Waa waa. The moral of the story? Never *ever* whine at the happiest place on earth.

Food for Thought

As mentioned earlier, Sonya Thomas may be
a petite little thing, but she can down quantities of food that would put Refrigerator
Perry to shame. Her multiple world records
are at best utterly frightening, and at worst
would keep the majority of us doing the
Technicolor yawn for months. You know
those nasty canned Armour Vienna sausages
that you only eat out of desperation? In 2005,
Thomas downed 8.31 pounds of those little
suckers in ten minutes. A year earlier, the
pint-sized gurgitator opted for dessert,
swallowing eleven pounds of cheesecake in
nine minutes. Nine minutes! And in 2006,
she put down forty-six crab cakes in ten
minutes. Oh, and paying mind to eating her
veggies, she also holds the record for deep-
fried okra. In 2006, she made short work of
9.75 pounds at the Oklahoma State Fair.
That took her all of ten minutes. That not
enough for you? How's about sixty-five hard-
boiled eggs in six minutes and forty seconds?
Almost thirty-two four-inch cheese quesa-
dillas in five minutes? Nine pounds of craw-
fish in ten minutes? It's inhuman.

The Dumb Jock Dictionary

Sports terms and what dimwit sportsers think they are!

Relief pitcher: *A glass of Pepto Bismol*

End zone: *The condition you're in when you can't pound down any more brewskis*

Triple Salchow: *A three-course meal at an Italian restaurant*

Oddball Athletics

Some avant-garde sports and the individuals who partake in them can be downright bizarre. This is one of those sports. The national sport of Afghanistan and Kyrgyzstan, *buskashi*, is a lot like polo only without the mallets. The upshot is that if you've got an abnormal hatred of goats, this might be the game for you. Buskashi fields two teams of horsemen who vie to carry a headless goat into the end zone of the opposing side. Worse yet, the game has no rules. It's arguably the most intense and dangerous game in the world, where goat carcasses get beaten to a pulp and deaths are commonplace. Tennis, anyone?

Scatterbrained Sportsters

One of the biggest sports stories in Japan in the summer of 2007, involved a scandal with Sumo grand champion Asashoryu. The twenty-six-year-old tough guy had just won the 21st Emperor's Cup—a prize that hundreds of wrestlers annually compete for—when he claimed injury and bowed out of a summer exhibition tournament. He even presented medical documents as proof that he needed time to heal from numerous injuries—or so he said. While he was supposed to be recovering, he was caught on tape playing a charity soccer event in Mongolia. Oops. Sumo grand champions are required to take their titles very seriously, always dressing the part, and avoiding controversy at all costs. Following the revelation that Asashoryu faked injury, the Japan Sumo Association suspended him for an unprecedented two tournaments and cut his pay by 30 percent for four months. What followed was equally shocking, with the distraught Asashoryu nearing nervous breakdown, barely able to speak, holding back tears, and begging to go back to his native Mongolia. But despite his depressive meltdown, the association denied his request and he quickly fell from grace. By all accounts, it was one helluva thud.

WHAT DO YOU CALL
A SINGLE BLONDE
WHO DRIVES A
LAMBORGHINI?

AN NBA PLAYER'S
EX - WIFE.

Who's on First?

One of the most controversial coaches in college basketball history is Bobby Knight, who led his NCAA Division One teams to more victories than any other head coach in the league. He's also raised more hackles and garnered more sketchy publicity than any other coach. After coaching Indiana University for twenty-nine years, Knight allegedly berated a freshman player and bruised the player's arm. The incident came on the heels of CNN reports that Knight had choked players during practices—news that ultimately proved too much for Indiana administrators. Knight was terminated in September of 2000. In addition, the Philistine also set women's rights back a few dozen years with an idiotically misogynistic comment made during an interview with Connie Chung in 1988. Referring to a basketball game where Knight felt referees were making biased calls against his Indiana team, he said: "I think if rape is inevitable, relax and enjoy it." With accusations of physically abusing his own players and stuffing his own foot into his mouth, Bobby Knight has managed to offset a stellar coaching career with a slew of stubbornly stupid and reprehensible gaffes. Mission accomplished, moron.

World Record Wackos

Anyone who follows soccer, recognized internationally as football, knows that top pros possess amazing skills when it comes to ball control, commonly bouncing soccer balls off their head and other body parts with astonishing accuracy. While bouncing a ball off your head can often be done for several minutes, it takes a determined individual to keep it up for much longer than that. Brazilian Martinho Eduardo Orige is just that person. In August of 2003, Orige bounced a regulation soccer ball on his head, legs, and feet for a whopping nineteen hours and thirty minutes. If you're thinking that it's no big deal, guess again. For the entire duration, Orige never let the ball touch the ground. Not to be outdone was Swede Tomas Lundman, who in February 2004 bounced a soccer ball off his head for eight hours, thirty-two minutes, and three seconds. That same year, Cuban Erick Hernández bounced a ball on his head 319 times in sixty seconds. Do you get the distinct impression that these guys have *way* too much time on their hands?

Nothing but Net!

Michael Vick:
www.imgoingtohell.org

Kobe Bryant:
www.igotawaywithit.com

Anna Kournikova:
www.imfullofmyself.com

What's in a Name?

The top ten NBA teams that never made it.

1. New York Knickers
2. Los Angeles Bakers
3. Washington Gizzards
4. San Antonio Slurs
5. Portland Snailblazers
6. Golden State Worriers
7. Denver McNuggets
8. Chicago Trolls
9. Boston Relics
10. Utah Spazz

Scatterbrained Sportsters

Can you imagine what public reaction would be if two prestigious football teams were headed to the Super Bowl, and the day before the big game one of the teams was thrown out of the league for steroid use? The entire team! That's essentially what happened to the French cycling team Festina in 1998 just before the annual Tour de France, which is as important to European sports nuts as the Super Bowl is to Americans. The debacle began when Festina's caretaker and masseur Willy Voet was arrested in France with a truckload of performance enhancing drugs and paraphernalia which put the entire team under a cloud of testosterone-soaked suspicion. Under grueling interrogations, all but two of the nine-member Festina team admitted to doping, which resulted in Tour de France director Jean-Maire Leblanc tossing the whole lot of them out of the race. Further investigations led to more doping suspicions and allegations about widespread drug use—enough so that the 1998 Tour de France earned the unfortunate nickname *Tour de Dopage*. What a buncha dopes.

Going Mental

Match the athletic neuroses to its prognosis.

1. Namathaphobia
2. Floydaphobia
3. Hammaphobia
4. Armstrongaphobia
5. Tonyaphobia
6. Knightaphobia
7. Alzadophobia
8. Juiceaphobia
9. Gretzaphobia
10. McMahonophobia

a. Fear of France
b. Fear of getting the crap beat out of you by your coach
c. Fear of gambling wives
d. Fear of pathological narcissists
e. Fear of drunk, grabby lechers
f. Fear of people not kissing your hiney
g. Fear of South Korea putting a hit on you
h. Fear of kneecaps and sex tapes
i. Fear of long-term steroid abuse
j. Fear of egomaniacs

Answers: 1-e, 2-a, 3-g, 4-j, 5-h, 6-b, 7-i, 8-d, 9-c, 10-f

Olympic Oops!

While we're utterly loath to include Greg
Louganis in a book about stupid athletes, it
stands to reason that what occurred at the
1988 Seoul Olympics was at best a serious
lack of judgment. The greatest diver of our
generation and arguably the best in diving
history, Louganis kept one helluva secret
going into the Games—one that sent the
media and the entire world into a tailspin.
Winning multiple world titles and gold medals in both springboard and tower at the
1984 Los Angeles Games, Louganis was a
heavy favorite in Seoul. But during the competition, disaster struck. While attempting a
reverse two-and-a-half pike Louganis hit
his head on the diving board, crashing to the
pool, and surfacing to reveal a bleeding
head. The cut forced him to reveal that he
was HIV positive, a revelation that for the
late eighties caused massive panic, with the
uninformed believing they could be infected
despite the fact that chlorine neutralizes the
virus. Once cleared by doctors, Louganis
pulled off what many consider the most
amazing comeback in sports history—he
performed a second dive to perfection and
won the gold.

WHAT'S THE DIFFERENCE
B E T W E E N
MICHAEL VICK
AND A CATFISH?

ONE'S A SCUM-SUCKING
BOTTOM FEEDER
AND THE OTHER'S
A FISH.

The Lobotomy Hall of Fame

Oh boy. Sometimes you've just gotta shake your head and wonder exactly how bloody daft certain sportsters are. Seriously. If they were any more stupid they'd have to be watered twice a week.

My sister's expecting a baby, and I don't know if I'm going to be an uncle or an aunt.
—North Carolina State hoopster Chuck Nevitt explaining to coach Jim Valvano why he was nervous at a 1982 practice

Tom.
—Newly hired Houston Rockets Tom Nissalke, when asked how he pronounced his name

I dunno. I never smoked any Astroturf.
—Tug McGraw when asked whether he preferred grass or Astroturf

Sure there have been injuries and deaths in boxing—but none of them serious.
—Boxer Alan Minter

There goes Juantorena down the back straight, opening his legs and showing his class.
—Commentator David Coleman at the 1976 Montreal Olympics

They shouldn't throw at me. I'm the father of five or six kids.
—Baseballer Tito Fuentes after getting hit by a pitch

Oddball Athletics

No doubt you've all attempted skipping stones across a scenic lake or pond, but we're guessing you've never attempted to huck a boulder into the drink. That's not the case for participants in a competition that has been going on since 1805—the historic *Unspunnen* Festival. One of the highlights of the fest, which is held in Interlaken, Switzerland, is the *Steintossen*, or stone throw event. In this case, however, the *Unspunnen* stone is a 184-pound chunk of granite that competitors raise above their heads. Taking a running start, they then heave the granite as far as they can. The 2006 winner, Markus Maire, threw the huge rock nearly thirteen feet. There's a joke in there about being caught between a rock and a hard place . . . but we won't go there.

Stupid Says . . .

66 Nobody has ever said anything about Marion Jones ever using performance-enhancing drugs and they never will. **99**
—Marion Jones

The Dumb Jock Dictionary

Sports terms and what dimwit sportsers think they are!

Homer: *Doh! Leader of* The Simpsons

Pommel horse: *Smacking a slow nag with a riding crop*

Intentional grounding: *What happens after the missus meets the mistress*

Fan Foolishness

People will sometimes do crazy things to get tickets to see their favorite team, but twenty-three-year-old Sarun Sharma did the extreme by offering his kidney for sale so that he could earn enough money to see his beloved Indian cricket team compete in the 2007 World Cup. Sharma was hoping to raise $7,000 to get to the West Indies, saying he wanted the cash in advance and would give his organ to the buyer upon his return. Sharma, a garment salesman, said he was too poor to pay for the trip on his own. "What's wrong with the offer?" said Sharma. "I know several people who are living with one kidney. My family cannot afford to fulfill my wishes." A few neighbors and friends tried to raise moola for his cause, but they couldn't even procure enough for a one-way ticket. Sadly, Sharma became the subject of relentless teasing which led him to consider suicide, telling the media he was considering jumping from the Mango bridge into the river Swarnarekha. After getting this information, police detained him, but later released him following observation. Which organ do you suppose he'd relinquish for Super Bowl tickets?

Bumper Snickers!

QUIT LAUGHING. YOUR DAUGHTER
MIGHT BE ONBOARD.
Wilt Chamberlain

QUIT BLEEPING FOLLOWING ME OR I'LL BLEEP
YOUR BLEEP AND THEN I'LL BLEEP YOUR
BLEEPING BLEEP. HAVE A NICE BLEEPING DAY.
Tommy Lasorda

Oddball Athletics

At one time or another we've all settled a
serious argument with a vicious game of
"Roshambo," otherwise known as Rock,
Paper, Scissors. But did you know that the
game has reached worldwide competition
levels with prize money reaching $50,000 for
the top spot? Fifty grand for Roshambo?
Who knew?

World Record Wackos

It isn't enough that watching a golf tournament is akin to watching paint dry. Oh no.
Along with one of the world's most boring
sports comes a host of ridiculous accouter-
ments not the least of which are plaid pants,
lime green sweaters, and hats any normal
human wouldn't be caught dead wearing,
save for David Arquette. That said, it should
come as no big shock that some guy's greatest ambition in life was to create the world's
longest golf cart. Similar to a limo, the *crème
de la crème* of golf cart luxury was created
by Peter Nee. It runs just over nineteen-
feet-long and includes a wine rack, bar,
stereo, and cigar humidor. Oh, and a DVD
player in case you need something to do
while waiting for your golf compadres to
recover their balls from the sand trap. This
is utterly stupid—par none.

Food for Thought

There's a time and place for eating certain foods and in most cases, those foods are accepted as part of competitive eating. Then there are other foods that most of us wouldn't touch unless we were forced or damn near starving to death. Not surprisingly, pro gurgitators don't possess that type of discretion. Beef tongue, for example, isn't on the average restaurant menu, but that matters little to Dominic Cardo, who consumed three pounds three ounces of beef tongue in a swift twelve minutes. And for those who are keeping score, the tongues were whole. Then there's Arturo Rios Jr., who in 2007 took only ten minutes to slop up close to three pounds of pig's feet and knuckles. And lest we forget, there's top gurgitator Takeru Kobayashi, who had no problem indulging in 17.7 pounds of cow brains in fifteen minutes. And if you're not reaching for your TUMS yet, take note of Richard LeFevre's Monty Python–esque tribute to SPAM. LeFevre managed to down six pounds of the canned mystery meat in twelve minutes. Let the TUMS commence. . . .

Running on Empty

At the 2004 Athens Olympics, twenty-two-year-old Justin Gatlin sprinted his way to a 100 meter gold medal, securing his status among the new generation of drug-free American athletes. As the USATF's poster boy for clean sport, Gatlin strongly touted the practice of running clean. That is until July 2006—a mere two months after setting the 100 meter world record—when he admitted testing positive for testosterone or its precursors. Oops. The messy battle that ensued had Gatlin's coach, Trevor Graham, claiming Gatlin's former masseur intentionally applied a testosterone cream to the sprinter during the Kansas City Relays meet in April. Lame! In college, Gatlin tested positive for Adderall which came as a result of ADD medication. That test stayed on-record. With the second infraction, he faced a lifetime ban unless he cooperated with the Feds and USADA officials in exchange for an eight-year ban. At his August 2007 arbitration hearing, Gatlin testified that Graham's assistant gave him anti-inflammatory pills and a vitamin B-12 shot two weeks before his positive test. Results are pending, but suffice to say his reign as world's fastest man was over in a split second.

The Über-Creepy Nibbler of the Century Award

Scoring off the charts on the icky meter is sports commentator Marv Alpert's sex life, which became tabloid fodder in 1997 after a ten-year relationship came to a horrific end. Among the many allegations of perversion were that Alpert had a penchant for wearing women's underwear while doing the nasty, and got his jollies engaging in forcible sodomy and back nibbling. Back *gnawing* to be exact. Alpert's protestations of innocence fell on deaf ears after DNA tests of the bite marks on his lover's back matched Alpert's choppers. Ultimately, the nasty nibbler was convicted of misdemeanor assault and battery for using his girlfriend as a chew toy and was given a twelve-month suspended sentence. NBC, for whom he'd worked for nearly twenty years, cut him loose, but two years later they reinstated him and he again became the NBA play-by-play man until broadcasting rights flipped over to ABC. Alpert still makes national appearances, but it's difficult to look at him without imagining him drooling in frilly unmentionables.

Baseball Boneheads

Some athletes give new meaning to the term
"dumb jock." This is one of those times. In
2002, reserve outfielder Ruben Rivera was
released by the New York Yankees after
stealing a bat and glove from teammate
Derek Jeter's locker and selling them to a
sports memorabilia dealer for $2,500. Rivera
returned the stolen items the next day, but it
was too late. His teammates unanimous-
ly voted to kick him off the team. Truth be
known, Rivera's career was filled with promise. The previous month he signed a one-year,
$1 million contract with the Yankees. Fol-
lowing the incident, the Yankees negotiated
a $200,000 settlement with Rivera. So why
would he make the stupid mistake of stealing something worth so little when he was
making so much dough? In a telephone
interview in his native Panama he said: "I
made a rookie's error. I did it without thinking, because it wasn't for the money. I had a
good contract. It was just an instant when I
wasn't thinking, and I made a mistake that
I'm paying for now." That's an $800,000 mis-
take for those who are counting.

WHAT'S THE DIFFERENCE
BETWEEN A HOCKEY PLAYER
AND A PARROT?

YOU CAN TEACH A
PARROT NOT TO
S W E A R .

Stupid Says . . .

❝I couldn't find London on a map if they didn't have the names of the countries. . . . I don't know what nothing is. I know Italy looks like a boot. . . . I know London Fletcher. . . . He's black, so I'm sure he's not from London. I'm sure that's a coincidental name.❞
—Dolphins linebacker Channing Crowder before a game in London

The Dumb Jock Dictionary

Sports terms and what dimwit sportsers think they are!

Balance beam: *The fine line between sobriety and a bottle of bourbon*

Tailgate: *A thong*

Southpaw: *Getting grabby with lap dancers below the Mason-Dixon Line*

Football Faux Pas

In 2007, twenty-two-year-old Mitch Cozad, a former backup punter for Northern Colorado, was convicted of second-degree assault and sentenced to seven years in prison for stabbing starter punter Rafael Mendoza in September 2006. Prosecutors alleged that Cozad was obsessed with getting the starting position, so he assaulted Mendoza outside his apartment, stabbing him with a five-inch-long knife in his kicking leg. Mendoza couldn't identify his attacker because he was dressed ninja-style, clad in black from head-to-toe; however, prosecutors portrayed Cozad as "an ambitious but frustrated athlete who stabbed Mendoza because he couldn't outplay him on the field." In addition, teammates and a friend testified that Cozad was bitter when he wasn't chosen as starter. He was acquitted of the more serious charge of attempted first-degree murder, which could've carried a sentence of up to forty-eight years. Mendoza went on to recover, playing ten games last season with plans to return the following season.

Bumper Snickers!

I'M NOT OBNOXIOUS.
I'M VERBALLY CHALLENGING.
John McEnroe

MY BITE IS WORSE THAN MY BARK.
Marv Alpert

Food for Thought

There are a few foods that one would never guess earn a spot in the record books when it comes to competitive eating. Take dumplings for example. Who knew that Cookie Jarvis ate ninety-one Chinese dumplings in eight minutes? Better yet, check out Dale Boone, who spent six minutes chowing down 274 Russian dumplings. That's insane. Who does that for sport? Then there's Richard LeFevre's record for eating birthday cake. Are you ready for this? Five pounds in eleven minutes. And if that weren't nuts enough, there's actually an IFOCE record for buffet food. The dubious distinction belongs to Crazy Legs Conti, who gobbled up five and a half pounds of buffet food in twelve minutes. He'd wreak havoc at an all-you-can-eat salad bar. . . .

Scatterbrained Sportsers

When you hear about something going horribly wrong at the racetrack it usually has something to do with gambling, fixing a race, or invigorating a poor equine with performance enhancing drugs. But that wasn't the case in 1990 at the Delta Downs racetrack in Louisana. It was a brutally foggy day when a group of jockeys hopped upon their trusty steeds to engage in a mile-long race. One of those jockeys was Sylvester Carmouche, who was riding Landing Officer, and running at 23-1 odds. The horses took off out of the gates but the fog proved impenetrable, until out of nowhere, Carmouche and Landing Officer crossed the finish line an astonishing twenty-four lengths ahead of the next horse and close to track record time. Twenty-four lengths? It didn't take long to ascertain that Carmouche dropped out of the race and conveniently positioned himself to reenter as the rest of the horses rounded the final turn. Problem was, the moron rejoined the race too soon. Idiot. For his amazing race, Carmouche won a ten-year ban, of which he served eight before rejoining jockeydom. No word on whether Landing Officer has recovered from the humiliation.

The Dumb Jock Dictionary

Sports terms and what dimwit sportsers think they are!

Foul tip: *Bad betting advice*

Shot put: *Committing murder*

Playoff: *When it's time for Viagra*

Oddball Athletics

In Mexico, there's an annual golf tournament that ain't on the PGA tour. It's the Elfego Baca Shoot, and it's a one-hole round that starts at the top of a 7,280-foot mountain peak and ends two and a half miles below. Participants aim their ball for the bottom of the mountain, and the first shot can travel as far as 600 yards. High altitude golf. This could possibly be the only time that golf could actually be more interesting than watching spackle dry. Wonder if any yetis have entered. . . .

WHY WERE **BASEBALL** PLAYERS GIVEN LARGER BRAINS THAN DOGS?

SO THEY WOULDN'T **H U M P** WOMEN'S LEGS AT COCKTAIL PARTIES.

Baseball Boneheads

Unlike most sports, it stands to reason that only in baseball can you get busted for bonking a bratwurst with a baseball bat. A home game tradition for the Milwaukee Brewers, their infamous Sausage Race is run after the end of the sixth inning as a promotion for Milwaukee's Klement's Sausage Co., with contestants dressing up in a variety of loopy rubber sausage-shaped costumes and racing around the field. But the spectacle went horribly pear-shaped in a July 2003 game against the Pittsburgh Pirates. Pirates first baseman Randall Simon took a misguided stab at humor by swatting a young woman—who was wearing the official Italian sausage outfit—with his favorite Louisville Slugger, sending her tumbling to the ground, and taking out the official hot dog runner in the process. Luckily, a kindly Polish sausage stopped and helped the hapless wieners to their feet so they could finish the race. Simon was actually arrested for assault, but charges were reduced to disorderly conduct, and he was fined $432 and suspended for the next three games. Thoughtfully, he signed the bat and gave it to the sausage lady as an apology. Pass the Grey Poupon. . . .

Basketball Buffoons

From 1994 to 1998 University of Minnesota hoopsters had it made in the shade when it came to academics. After an eight-month investigation into basketball coach Clem Haskins's involvement in a cheating scandal, it turned out the university's academic counseling department was preparing the course work for most of the team's star players. Haskins denied any involvement, but after eighteen players were grilled, there was little question that they weren't bothering to do their homework. In fact, many of them weren't even showing up for class. What did they do with all that spare time? More than likely, spending all the cash payments they were being slipped under the table. In 2002, Minnesota courts ordered Haskins to cough up more than $800,000. The basketball team was slapped with a four-year probation by the NCAA. Nice play, coach!

Oddball Athletics

It's no mystery that there are sports in which participants risk their lives, for example skydiving, bungee jumping, NASCAR, and skating competitions involving Tonya Harding. But for the truly masochistic athlete who thrives on pure torture, there is only one option: England's Tough Guy competition. At first glance, the contest appears to be a sort of foot race, but it quickly goes to hell. After a basic run of about 4,000 meters, competitors hit the obstacle course, charmingly named the "killing fields," which includes underground and underwater tunnels, fire pits, electric fences, barbed wire, and flesh-shredding nettle patches. Organizers gleefully claim that once you've entered, you've signed your own death warrant. Line forms to the left for interested parties. . . .

Stupid Says . . .

❝I didn't kill nobody; I didn't rape no children; I had sex with a woman who wasn't my wife. It was wrong, but I paid for it.❞

—Boris Becker

The Dumb Jock Dictionary

Sports terms and what dimwit sportsers think they are!

On the ropes: *An S&M session*

Épée: *What you have to do in a cup before games*

Hurler: *The winner of a professional mayonnaise-eating competition*

Stupid Says . . .

66That's what I call the ultimate
laxative.99

—Canadian Prime Minister of
Sports Otto Jelinek, after riding
the luge down the
Winter Olympics course

Food for Thought

My bologna has a first name. It's G-R-O-S-S.
Oops. Apologies to Oscar Meyer. It couldn't
be helped, especially after learning that
there does indeed exist a world record for
eating America's favorite faux meat substance. The dubious distinction is held by
Don Lerman, who in 2006 spent six long
minutes of his life shoving more than two
and three quarter pounds of pork and
chicken bologna down his gullet. He's a
brave man that Don Lerman. A very brave
man. . . .

Running on Empty

At the 2004 Athens Olympics, the most anticipated sprint event for the Greeks was the
men's 200 meters, in which the country's hero,
Kostas Kenteris, was to defend his gold
medal title from the 2000 Sydney Games.
What would turn out to be the dominant
story of the Games was the insane debacle
involving Kenteris and his training partner,
Sydney 100 meter silver medalist Katerina
Thanou. Turns out, they decided to play hide-
and-seek with drug testers for several
months prior to and on the eve of the opening
ceremonies, telling a ridiculous story involving a motorcycle crash, miscommunication
with their coach about testing times, and a
host of suspicious events and excuses that
plummeted them into the annals of Olympic
disgrace and resulted in their being banned
from the Games. The Greek citizenry were
crushed and deeply embarrassed, especially
considering Kenteris was rumored to be the
one lighting the Olympic flame. In 2006, both
were reinstated after enduring a messy battle,
suspension, and connection to the BALCO
scandal. Presumed guilty despite never having tested positive, the pair added yet another
permanent stain on the already chaotically
polluted sport of track and field.

WHAT IS TEN MILES
LONG AND HAS AN
I.Q. OF SIXTY?

AN NHL PARADE.

Olympic Oops!

The 2004 Athens Olympics had its share of top notch controversies, another of which was a supreme scoring screw-up in men's gymnastics that gave American Paul Hamm a controversial All-Around gold medal win over South Korea's Yang Tae Young, who was inaccurately docked a tenth of a point before he began the parallel bars rotation. The starting difficulty point should have been 10.0 instead of the 9.9 the judges scored from, and the difference in value made the final scoring the difference between first place to third. The gaffe set off a firestorm of speculation that Hamm would have to forfeit the medal to Young. The error was so glaring the International Gymnastics Federation suspended three judges who refused to admit their mistake. Appeals by South Korea fell on deaf ears and Hamm, along with his lack of sportsmanship, kept his controversial medal. One minor bit of justice to come out of the mess was that General Mills made deals with winning U.S. Olympians to put their images on boxes of Wheaties—with the notable exception of Hamm. After all, it's the breakfast of champions, not the breakfast of chumps.

The Scoreboard

Another ten sports movie sequels that never made it:

1. *Hoop Screams*
2. *The Nair up There*
3. *The Plumber's Wife*
4. *Bagels in the Outfield*
5. *The Unnatural*
6. *Remember the Tritons*
7. *The Black Scallion*
8. *Friday Night Tights*
9. *Spend It Like Beckham*
10. *Brian's Thong*

The Dumb Jock Dictionary

Sports terms and what dimwit sportsers think they are!

Triple crown: *A really bad tooth*

Uneven bars: *What the jail cell looks like when you're tossed into the pokey for DUI*

Grand slam: *A misdemeanor*

World Record Wackos

One of the most anticipated premier sports events is arguably the running of the 100 meters, a race giving title to the "World's Fastest Man." The current world record is held by Jamaica's Asafa Powell who, on September 9, 2007, ran it in a blazing 9.74 seconds. That said, we're guessing that you've never heard of Dutchman Nico Surings, but he's also one of the world's fastest 100 meter runners—only his record is for running the distance on ice and barefoot. On December 8, 2006, the barefoot wonder that *is* Nico Surings set his world record in Eindhoven, Netherlands, in 17.35 seconds. No word on how long it took for his tootsies to defrost.

Scatterbrained Sportsters

In 2006, for the first time in the history of cycling's most illustrious event, a Tour de France winner was stripped of his title for doping offenses. The horrific honor went to American Floyd Landis, who steadfastly denied ever having used steroids at any point in his career. Uh huh. Science and the U.S. Anti-Doping Agency conclusively proved otherwise and slapped Landis with a two-year suspension and a shameful legacy that will never be repaired, no matter how many indignant pleas of innocence the embattled cyclist sputters. Australian wheeler Stuart O'Grady first had suspicions during the race when at one point he was a full thirteen minutes ahead of Landis. Then the American suddenly blew past like he was standing still. After putting Landis' urine samples through two separate laboratory tests, there was little question that his testosterone level was better than twice the normal limit. The ridiculous nature of his doping is that under increasingly controlled conditions and oversight, the testing for steroids is virtually foolproof—which points to the simple fact that Landis was unequivocally proven a cheat. For shame Mr. Landis. For shame. . . .

Could They Be Any Dumber?

Match the moronic athlete with their bad behavior.

a. Tim Montgomery   **e.** Martina Hingis
b. Larisa Lazutina   **f.** Mike Danton
c. Tyler Hamilton   **g.** Danny Almonte
d. Rosie Ruiz   **h.** Tim Hardaway

1. Tested positive for blood doping after winning a cycling gold medal, but kept his medal when his second sample was inadvertently frozen. Wasn't so lucky in 2007.
2. Tested positive for cocaine and immediately retired.
3. Cheated during the 1980 Boston Marathon.
4. Busted for a multmillion-dollar bank fraud and money laundering scheme.
5. Little League World Series winner who lied about his age.
6. Arrested in conjunction with a murder-for-hire plot.
7. Was fired and disgraced after professing homophobia and unleashing an anti-gay rant.
8. Famed cross-country skier banned from the 2002 Olympics for doping.

Answers:
1-c, 2-e, 3-d,
4-a, 5-g, 6-f,
7-h, 8-b

Jailbird Jocks

Professional jocks have a bizarre habit of
ruining perfectly good multimillion-dollar
careers by pulling idiotic stunts, and former
Chicago Bears defensive tackle Tank Johnson is no exception. Since he was drafted in
1995, Johnson managed to get himself
arrested five times, and had ten friendly little "chats" with police officers about other
incidents. It seems the six-foot-three 300
pounder lacks faith in his imposing physique, choosing to supplement his intimida-
tion by collecting loads of firearms.
Johnson's slide began in 2005 outside a Chicago nightclub where he was arrested for
possessing an illegal handgun. After taking
a plea deal, Johnson was put on probation
for eighteen months, but apparently couldn't
take the hint and was arrested again in 2006
after Chicago police raided his home and
found enough loaded assault weapons to
start a small-scale war. That error in judgment won Johnson a forty-five day vacation
in the Cook County Jail. After the conviction, the Bears finally had enough of Johnson's firearms fetish and cut him from the
squad. Maybe the guy should just join the
Marines.

Basketball Buffoons

Sadly, there are more than a few NBA players who over the years have proved that they're not the sharpest tools in the shed. Count Isiah Thomas as one of those idiots. As a Detroit Piston who was part of the team who lost to the Boston Celtics in the 1987 Eastern Conference finals, Thomas despicably uttered: "If Larry Bird were black, he'd be just another good guy." That comment, among other incidents, created a firestorm of controversy and painted Thomas as a racist. Fast forward to the Fall of 2007, where Thomas, who's now coach of the New York Knicks, was playing center in a judicial court after he, Steve Mills, and Madison Square Garden CEO James Dolan faced charges of sexual harassment brought on in 2006 by former Garden senior vice president Anucha Browne Sanders. Thomas was singled out by Browne Sanders as having made sexual advances, racist remarks, and verbal insults. After a three-week trial, Madison Square Garden was ordered to pay Browne Sanders over $11 million—one of the largest sexual harassment settlements in history. That oughta get their knickers in a twist.

The Nauseating Narcissists of the Decade Award

Why is it that some American athletes feel the need to taint the rest of us Yanks with obscene bursts of horrendous sportsmanship? Case in point, the 2000 Sydney Games and egomaniacs Jon Drummond, Bernard Williams, Brian Lewis, and former "world's fastest man" Maurice Greene. After the quartet won track and field's coveted 4x100 meter relay, they embarked on a disgraceful lack of humility that managed to anger not only Americans, but damn near everyone on the planet. Taking a victory lap, the peabrained quicksters began posing, flexing, preening, making faces, and acting like supreme jerks. Two of them even stripped their shirts and wrapped themselves in the Stars and Stripes. It was an unforgivable display of narcissism that extended to the podium, where they postured, played with their medals, and made bizarre faces. Greene even stuck his tongue at the cameras. Sickening. In 2004, prior to the Athens games, the United States took the wise step of briefing Olympians on public conduct, but it was too late for the world's fastest quartet, who left their mark as some of the worst Olympic gold medal winners of all time.

The Dumb Jock Dictionary

Sports terms and what dimwit sportsers think they are!

Round Robin: *Team mascot at the local strip joint*

Face-off: *When the window slides shut at the peep show booth*

Wide receiver: *A blondie waitress with junk in the trunk*

Bumper Snickers!

I'M REALLY EASY TO GET ALONG WITH ONCE PEOPLE LEARN TO WORSHIP ME.
Nancy Kerrigan

THERE ARE FIVE KINDS OF PLAYERS. THOSE WHO WIN, AND THOSE WHO DON'T.
Yogi Berra

Food for Thought

For us mere mortals, the consumption of corned beef is generally limited to deli sandwiches and St. Patrick's Day. Not so for intrepid gurgitators. Known as "the People's Champ" for his multitude of world records and consistent standing with the IFOCE, Eric Booker is a fan favorite. At 420 pounds, the thirty-seven-year-old New Yorker elevated corned beef hash to world record heights when he annihilated four pounds in one minute and fifty-eight seconds. Of equal repute is twenty-two-year-old Patrick Bertoletti, whose fondness for corned beef apparently knows no bounds. In 2006, he downed eleven eight-ounce corned beef sandwiches in ten minutes. Yikes. A year later, he upped the ante and laid waste to more than ten and a half pounds of corned beef and cabbage, also in ten minutes. Irishmen everywhere are hyperventilating as we speak.

Oddball Athletics

Archers who possess the desire to kill, but who don't have the stomach to go through with bloodshed now have an intriguing sporting option—they can take part in nonviolent 3-D tournaments held throughout the United States by the National Field Archer's Association. If you're interested, you can sight-in on life-sized dummies of wild pigs, turkeys, and deer that you can drill to your heart's content with nary a squeal. Bambi would be very proud.

Scatterbrained Sportsters

It was Fight Night on December, 8, 2001, but it didn't take place in a boxing ring—it happened in a hockey rink when the Calgary Flames faced off with the Anaheim Mighty Ducks in what could more accurately be termed a brawl than a hockey game. During the roughhousing, wherein actual hockey was periodically played, there were ten full-on fights, with eight of them happening in a mere nine seconds. The Ducks won the game 4-0, but in reality, the game went to the refs, who scored exponentially more points by calling more than 300 minutes worth of penalties. And you wonder why hockey players are missing teeth?

WHY DO
DUMB JOCKS
PREFER BLONDES?

BECAUSE THEY ENJOY INTELLECTUAL EQUALS.

Who's on First?

Professional baseball seems to have one consistent goal that began the day the game was invented—setting records and breaking them as quickly as possible. In July of 2002, the Tampa Rays's farm team, the Charleston Riverdogs, set a record for pro baseball's lowest attendance with an audience of zero. Nada. Zilch. In truth, the pathetic turnout was part of a media stunt dreamed up by play-by-play announcer Jim Lucas, who talked team owners into keeping fans locked out of the stadium until the game was declared official after five full innings of play. Instead, fans milled around outside the park, peering through fences and gates, with some using stepladders to watch the action over the barricades. The previous attendance record is disputed, but announcer Lucas claims that a Chicago game had an attendance of twelve courageous souls who braved a horrific rainstorm on September 17, 1881. The Riverdogs hope to sneak past that one but, according to baseball rules, season ticket holders will count as paid attendance— whether they could get in or not. Fittingly, the theme song for the Riverdogs's game was the Beatles's hit *Nowhere Man*.

World Record Wackos

You know that big awkward piece of
machinery that's collecting dust in the cor-
ner of your living room? Yeah, that's it, the
one you use for drying your underwear. Well
believe it or not, there are several world
records involving that dreaded treadmill, set
by a few folks who no doubt need their heads
examined. For starters, there's Hungarian
gal Edit Berces who took to a treadmill at a
Budapest shopping mall in March 2004. In
twenty-four hours, Ms. Berces logged in
153.6 miles. Not to be outdone by the fairer
sex, American Christopher Bergland took
up the challenge a month later in New York,
setting the male version of the bizarre treadmill record by covering 153.76 miles also in
twenty-four hours. Something says these
two should become gym partners.

The Dumb Jock Dictionary

Sports terms and what dimwit sportsers think they are!

High bar: *What a saloon looks like to a midget wrestler*

Goal post: *A MySpace blog*

Touchback: *The safest way to fondle a stripper without getting slapped*

Nothing but Net!

Bobby Riggs:
www.iplaylikeagirl.org

Wade Boggs:
www.adulterers.org

David Beckham:
www.imricherthangod.org

What's in a Name?

The top ten National Hockey League teams that never made it.

1. Houston Soilers
2. Los Angeles Queens
3. Boston Ruins
4. Toronto Maple Reefers
5. San Jose Snarks
6. Detroit Buffalo Wings
7. New Jersey Navels
8. Phoenix Peyotes
9. Philadelphia Criers
10. New York Bingers

Olympic Oops!

The 1996 Atlanta Games saw its share of controversy, not the least of which was a pipe bomb exploding in Centennial Olympic Park that killed two people. But in the pool, there was a different kind of explosion going on in the form of Irishwoman Michelle Smith, who garnered three gold medals and one bronze. Ireland, not known for its swimming contenders, had a new national hero, as Smith became the first Irish woman to ever win Olympic gold. But as with all heroes there came the inevitable downfall. In 1994, Smith began training under future hubby Erik de Bruin, a Dutch shot putter and discus thrower who served a four-year ban for testosterone use. As a result, suspicion of drug use ran high for Smith in Atlanta given her extraordinary times, consistent wins on the international circuit, and her huge leap in world rankings. Smith passed her Olympic drug tests, but in January of 1998 a random out-of-competition urine test contained enough whiskey to kill a human and ultimately mask drug use. A second test in May showed similar results after which Smith was handed a four-year ban for alleged tampering. Shot of Jack, anyone?

Going Mental

Match the athletic neuroses to its prognosis.

1. Bradyphobia
2. Dukelacrossaphobia
3. Gatlinaphobia
4. Kournikovaphobia
5. Kobeaphobia
6. Lasordaphobia
7. Roseaphobia
8. Marionaphobia
9. Beckaphobia
10. McEnroeaphobia

a. Fear of vindictive masseurs
b. Fear of irrational outbursts
c. Fear of flaxseed oil
d. Fear of Mike Nifong
e. Fear of really bad haircuts
f. Fear of being obscenely rich
g. Fear of believing you're God's gift to maledom
h. Fear of dumping your baby mama for a supermodel
i. Fear of expletives
j. Fear of sexual assault charges

*Answers: 1-h,
2-d, 3-a, 4-g,
5-j, 6-i, 7-e,
8-c, 9-f, 10-b*

Scatterbrained Sportsters

Pro wrestling's sketchy record of encouraging steroid use among its superstars came under intense scrutiny on June 25, 2007, after the bodies of Chris Benoit, his wife Nancy, and their seven-year-old son David were found dead in their Georgia home in what was obviously a murder/suicide committed by the wildly popular wrestling legend once known as the "Canadian Crippler." Accusations of 'roid rage prompted investigations into steroid abuse in every level of professional wrestling, resulting in twelve WWE superstars being suspended in a highly publicized attempt to quell growing media attention. In the end, neurosurgeons at West Virginia University determined that severe damage to Benoit's brain caused by repeated concussions in the ring resulted in what was described as "the brain of an eighty-five-year-old Alzheimer's patient." From the evidence, it appeared Benoit's break with reality was caused by dementia and depression. It's a sad ending to a superstar who made his fortune in a sport that specializes in breaks from reality. But seriously. With all the head bashing and steroid abuse, who didn't see this coming?

HOW MANY
LINEMEN
DOES IT TAKE TO POP
POPCORN?

THREE.
ONE TO HOLD THE PAN
AND TWO OTHERS
TO SHAKE THE STOVE.

Dennis the Menace

We all know that former NBA hoopster Dennis Rodman is a unique fellow, one who has no problem expressing his individuality. Alright. We lie. He's scary. In truth, it's not the tats or the piercings or his nanosecond nuptials to Carmen Electra or even the wacky hair or penchant for bridal wear. It's what comes out of his mouth.

"To hang out in a gay bar or put on a sequined halter top makes me feel like a total person.**"**

"Chemistry is a class you take in high school or college, where you figure out two plus two is ten, or something.**"**

"If I want to wear a dress, I'll wear a dress.**"**

"I say I'm Jimi Hendrix, Jim Morrison, Janis Joplin all wrapped up into one. If I die early . . . I'll be just like those guys.**"**

"As long as I play ball, I can get any woman I want.**"**

Oddball Athletics

Crazy as it may sound, one of most unusual
sports on the planet is unicycle hockey,
which is played with ice hockey sticks, a ball,
and of course, unicycles. Believe it or not,
there are national leagues all over the world
and even an International Unicycling Federation that publishes all the rules and regula-
tions. Unicycles. They aren't just for circuses
anymore. Who knew?

The Dumb Jock Dictionary

Sports terms and what dimwit sportsers
think they are!

Pinch hitter: *Assault and battery charges*

Racket: *Perky* Girls Gone Wild *hooters*

Tight end: *The view you have walking
behind a Dallas Cowboys cheerleader*

Scatterbrained Sportsters

Have you ever heard of Dora Ratjen? How about Hermann Ratjen? Doesn't ring any bells? Well, Dora was a world class high jumper who competed in the 1936 Berlin Olympics. Hermann was an ordinary bloke who was working as a waiter in Hamburg, Germany after World War II. Were they related? You bet. Dora and Hermann were one and the same. What in the world possessed Hermann to compete as a chick? And why wasn't he busted? According to Hermann, the Hitler Youth leaders of the era pressured him into putting the kibosh on his cojones and literally play like a girl. Sadly, Dora couldn't live up to her pressured coercion, placing fourth in the competition. Had they been testing for Nair or Aqua Velva, no doubt Dora's cover would've been blown!

Fan Foolishness

In 2002, Kansas City Royals first base coach Tom Gamboa was focused on a game against the Chicago White Sox when two fans ran onto the field and attacked him. Thirty-four-year-old William Ligue Jr. and his fifteen-year-old son rushed Gamboa and started beating him, as the Royals raced to help. After the fight, police found a pocketknife that one of the White Sox saw fall out of the crazed fan's pocket. After being arrested for aggravated battery, the disruptive duo said they'd had an exchange with Gamboa, claiming he flipped off the son. According to the father, Gamboa "got what he deserved." Nice. Gamboa, who sustained cuts, bruises and some hearing loss, denied the exchange saying he'd "never at any time ever verbally or physically acknowledged the people in the stands and I encourage players to just tune them out." Lingue received thirty months probation, with his son receiving five. But in 2006, daddy dearest broke probation for a 2004 offense of breaking into a car and leading police on a chase and was slapped with almost five years in the pokey. Great role model, eh?

Oddball Athletics

One of the loopiest sports on the planet is called *kadabbi*, a team sport of seven players each whom play on a twelve-and-a-half by ten-meter court. Wacky as it may sound, the game is played by alternately sending a single competitor into the other team's half of the court to tag as many opponents as he can and return to his half—all in one breath. To prove it, he must chant "kabaddi" continually without stopping to breathe. Believe it or not, the sport has ancient roots and is said to have been demonstrated at the 1936 Olympics in Berlin. You just can't make this stuff up.

Stupid Says . . .

❝I quit school in the sixth grade because of pneumonia. Not because I had it, but because I couldn't spell it.**❞**
—Boxer Rocky Graziano

World Record Wackos

Unless we're seriously mistaken, it's fair to say that there's no one on the planet who truly loves doing push-ups. No one. No matter how much they fib and tell you they do. That said, it must be noted that Canadian Doug Pruden is nuts. Why, you ask? Because he holds the world record for doing push-ups. Set in July of 2005, Pruden did 1,781 push-ups in sixty minutes. And just to add wonderment to this already insane accomplishment, please know that he did them using the back of his hands. Told ya he was nuts. . . .

Food for Thought

Arguably the premier event and most coveted world record among competitive eaters is the hot dog title. Considered by many to be the dominant gurgitator in the world is twenty-nine-year-old Takeru Kobayashi. Weighing in at 160 pounds and representing his home country of Japan, Kobayshi's talents are legendary and his successes have made him the guy to beat. In 2006, the king of dogs won his sixth consecutive title at Coney Island, consuming almost fifty-four Nathan's Famous Hot Dogs and the buns in a blazing twelve minutes. On July 4, 2007, however, Kobayashi's reign of beefy terror came to an end when he was defeated by Joey Chestnut, who downed sixty-six dogs in twelve minutes. The two remain at the top of their game and in constant battle. Kobayashi continues to hold several records, including cow brains, rice balls (twenty in thirty minutes), lobster rolls (forty-one in ten minutes), and an astonishing performance when eating Johnsonville Brats. He ate fifty-eight in ten minutes.

Running on Empty

You may not recognize the name Rosie Ruiz, but in 1980, the twenty-three-year-old New Yorker ran the third fastest time a woman had ever run in the Boston Marathon. It was an astonishing victory made all the more shocking by the fact that she was so quick that no one actually saw her run the race, and no cameras or monitors captured her image. As such, a cloud of suspicion immediately fell over Ruiz, who didn't appear the least bit tired or worse for wear when she accepted her accolades. Days later the Ruiz hoax was uncovered, and it was a doozy. Ruiz apparently started the race but dropped out and boarded a subway that took her about a mile from the finish. She simply rejoined the race, and sprinted in for a grand victory. She qualified for the race with her time from the 1979 New York Marathon, which was erased after it was learned she also used the subway to complete that race. In 1982, she was arrested for grand larceny and forgery to the tune of $60,000, and a year later was incarcerated for peddling coke to undercover cops.

The Ski Bunny from Hell Award

Aspen, Colorado, is a Mecca for ski buffs, ski bums, and filthy rich celebrities who love blasting down the slopes at breakneck speeds. Unfortunately for local boy Vladimir "Spider" Sabich, who became a two-time World Champion in the early seventies, his last blast was a fatal bullet fired in his Aspen home on March 21, 1976, by B-list celebrity Claudine Longet. Up until then, Longet's sketchy claim to fame was her marriage to beloved singer Andy Williams, who dumped her after a tumultuous six-year relationship. After that, she and Sabich fell head over heels in lust and lived together for two years. The murder trial against Longet turned into a mess of O.J. proportion, with bungled evidence and sloppy prosecution. Longet's claims to have accidentally killed Sabich while he was showing her his pistol played into the jury's sympathies, although locals knew that Sabich had every intention of ending the relationship. Longet was convicted of negligent homicide and served a paltry thirty days in the slammer. Said Sabich's father: "Claudine accomplished only two things—marrying Andy Williams and getting away with murder."

WHAT'S THE DIFFERENCE BETWEEN BOBBY KNIGHT AND CHILDBIRTH?

ONE CAN BE TERRIBLY PAINFUL AND UNBEARABLE WHILE THE OTHER IS JUST HAVING A BABY.

Baseball Boneheads

It was a mismatch from the get-go when Red Sox pitching ace Pedro Martinez threw seventy-two-year-old Yankees bench coach Don Zimmer to the ground during a brawl that ensued at a 2003 championship game at Yankee Stadium. The sordid debacle began when Martinez fired a pitch that barely missed Yankee Karim Garcia's noggin, giving Garcia a free ride to first base. Garcia then made a break for second on the next ball hit and flattened second baseman Todd Walker, which started a shoving bout between the two irate players and got everybody on their feet in a belligerent shouting match. After calming down a bit, the Yankees took to the field at the bottom of the inning, and all was well until pitcher Roger Clemens blistered a fastball that nearly nailed Manny Ramirez, causing both sides to angrily storm the field. That was when the aged but sprightly Zimmer took a run at Martinez, who easily tossed him to the dirt. Zimmer had no comment about getting flattened by a youngster half his age except to say: "We won the game!" Baseballers are a bizarre lot. Clearly they've taken too many fastballs to the frontal lobe.

Olympic Oops!

Still reeling from the infamous bribery scandal, the last thing organizers of the 2002 Salt Lake City Games needed was further controversy. But that's exactly what happened after Canadian figure skating pairs team Jamié Sale and David Pelletier lost to Russia's Elena Berezhnaya and Anton Sikharulidze. Any idiot could see that the Russian team's performance contained at least six flaws, including a stumbling side-by-side double Axel, while Canada's duo was near perfect. When the scores appeared, Salé and Pelletier were visibly stunned as the crowd of 16,000 exploded in a cacophony of shocked boos and hisses. The nine judges awarded the win to the Russians 5-4, but it was clear that someone fixed the judging. After the medal ceremony, the spotlight turned to French judge Marie-Reine Le Gougne, who sided with the bloc of judges from Russia, China, Poland, and Ukraine, who were inherently predisposed toward the Russians. Known as "SkateGate," Le Gougne admitted to trading votes in exchange for favorable scoring for French ice-dancing pairs. She was booted in disgrace from Olympic judging, and a second set of gold medals were belatedly awarded to the Canadians.

Stupid Says . . .

"It isn't like I came down from Mount Sinai with the tabloids.**"**
—Former Indianapolis Colts coach Ron Meyer

The Dumb Jock Dictionary

Sports terms and what dimwit sportsers think they are!

Double play: *A pair of strumpets*

Batter up: *Mark McGwire testifying before a Senate Investigations Committee*

Drag strip: *A transvestite red light district*

Football Faux Pas

Seventeen pro football players created their own version of "Boys Gone Wild" on October 6, 2005, when key members of the Minnesota Vikings piled into two rented yachts and sailed around Lake Minnetonka with enough booze and hookers to make Hugh Hefner blush. An estimated ninety partygoers plied the waters, but it appears the only sights worth seeing were inside the boats. According to a charter cruise employee who witnessed the smutty affair there was plenty of action: "Woman on man, woman on woman, toys, middle of the floor, middle of the couches, middle of the room." Holy lovefest, Batman! The hapless cleaning crew probably should've called in a Hazmat team, considering the boats were littered with a sticky amalgam of used condoms, wrappers, tubes of lubricant, Handi Wipes, and sex toy packaging. Of the seventeen footballers involved in the bonk-fest, Fred Smoot, Moe Williams, and Bryant McKinnie took the heat for the nautical naughtiness and got stuck with convictions for disorderly conduct. We applaud the clean-up crew for tidying up the Love Boat from Hell.

Food for Thought

If you suffer from heartburn, please take a Pepcid before you continue reading. (We're not kidding.) There's no doubt that any individual participating in the sport of competitive eating has an iron stomach, but some food records are beyond belief. For a trio of seasoned food vets acid reflux must not be an issue, because each holds a record involving a major perpetrator: the jalapeño. The year 2006 proved fruitful for the hot little pepper. On April 8, Joey Chestnut spent a mere ten minutes consuming 118 jalapeño poppers at the University of Arizona. Four months later, on August 26, Patrick Bertoletti visited the Sky City Casino where he offed 177 pickled jalapeños in fifteen minutes. And on October 8, Richard LeFevre attended the Texas State Fair, where he took on the category of short-form pickled jalapeños, downing 247 in an astonishing eight minutes. Don't say we didn't warn you. . . .

Scatterbrained Sportsters

One of the most infamous pro wrestling dimwits is "Stone Cold" Steve Austin, who began his ascent to superstardom in 1996 in a famous battle with Jake "The Snake" Roberts, who'd taken on a role as a Bible verse quoting born-again. Before the bout, Roberts made a reference to John 3:16 and, after Austin thoroughly trounced Roberts in the ring, Austin mouthed off with a victorious phrase that made him famous: "Talk about your John 3:16. Austin 3:16 says I just whooped your ass!" The comment triggered an advertising and marketing blitz, and "Austin 3:16" T-shirts sold by the tens of thousands, making the bobbleheaded brawler an icon. Plagued with a serious neck injury and burning through three wives, the last of whom had Austin arrested for domestic abuse in 2002, he eventually fell out of favor as a WWE top draw, instead relegated to increasingly stupid storylines. Case in point, an infamous incident where he delivered his signature "stunner" move to an eighty-year-old female wrestler. Eighty. What kind of creep beats up little old ladies for fun? Stone Cold Jerkwad.

Bumper Snickers!

QUIT HONKING. I'M RELOADING.
Darryl Strawberry

MY SON IS INMATE OF THE MONTH!
Ruby Strawberry

The Dumb Jock Dictionary

Sports terms and what dimwit sportsers think they are!

Shortstop: *A quick brothel visit*

Hacky Sack: *A city in New Jersey*

Testosterone: *An Italian sports car*

Oddball Athletics

A relatively new addition to the Winter
Olympics is skeleton, an incredibly dangerous backward form of luge that leaves you
wondering if participants have a serious
death wish. Of course, those folks are all
pros. Not so for individuals who participate
in street luge, where you lie on your back on
a long board with wheels and fly down steep
inclines *feet first*. Strictly gravity driven,
street lugers can hit speeds of more than
seventy miles an hour, and in case you're
curious, yes, spectacular crashes are commonplace. Anyone up for a race?

WHAT IS GROSS STUPIDITY?

TWENTY-EIGHT HOCKEY PLAYERS IN A LOCKER ROOM.

Baseball Boneheads

Of all the loudmouthed chumps to play major league baseball, Jose Canseco stands out as the most self-aggrandizing backstabber to stink up the sport, particularly after he retired from the majors in 2001. In his 2005 tell-all autobiography *Juiced: Wild Times, Rampant 'Roids, Smash Hits, and How Baseball Got Big*, Canseco described his regular use of steroids and dragged a half-dozen other superstars into the sordid world of sports doping while also implicating 85 percent of *all* ball players. In doing so, the bird-brained former outfielder set himself up to be an altruistic whistleblower and proved himself to be little more than a petty publicity hound with a sketchy past. The book's publication triggered a congressional inquiry into steroid use that turned MLB on its ear, and cast doubts on every major athlete in nearly every major sport. Canseco's lurid accusations may have a serious impact on his Hall of Fame chances, which San Francisco sports writer Bruce Jenkins noted when he said: "The last ten years people have been laughing at him. Hall of Famers are not the object of scorn." Scorn indeed. . . .

Lamest Excuse of the Decade Award

American sprinter Dennis Mitchell, who won the 4x100 relay in the 1992 Barcelona Olympics, failed drug tests in 1998 for excessive levels of testosterone. In one of the more classic excuses, he reasoned that his positive test was due to consuming five bottles of beer and having sex four times the night before the test. The IAAF didn't care about his sex life and banned Mitchell from competition for two years. If you're keeping tabs on his two-year ban, it amounts to 2,920 sex sessions.

Stupid Says . . .

66Half this game is ninety percent mental.99
—Philadelphia Phillies manager
Danny Ozark

The Dumb Jock Dictionary

Sports terms and what dimwit sportsers think they are!

Shuttlecock: *The way NBAers get from their hotel to the stadium*

Skins Game: *The Nudist Super Bowl*

Pass interference: *Getting dumped before last call*

Nothing but Net!

Joe Namath:
www.seriallechers.org

Ben Johnson:
www.liarliarpantsonfire.com

Wilt Chamberlain:
www.isleptwitheveryone.com

Basketball Buffoons

During a radio interview in early 2007, former NBA Miami Heat point guard and five-time All-Star Tim Hardaway made vile homophobic comments that got him crucified by the media and snubbed by the NBA. The diatribe came on the heels of former NBA center John Amaechi coming out of the closet several years after retiring. Said Hardaway: "Well, you know, I hate gay people. I let it be known I don't like to be around gay people. It shouldn't be in the world. . . ." Yikes! While the media was busy raking Hardaway for the crass commentary, Commissioner David Stern banished him from their annual All-Star Weekend in Las Vegas, saying: "we didn't think his comments were consistent with having anything to do with us." Back-peddling as fast as he could, Hardaway's agent issued a statement of apology, saying Hardaway was sorry for causing embarrassment to his fans and the NBA. Amaechi, who is only the sixth professional out of the four major leagues (hockey, baseball, basketball, and football) to come out, didn't quite buy Hardaway's feeble attempt at quelling the firestorm. We don't buy it either.

Food for Thought

Ah . . . a burger and fries. Sounds good on occasion, don't it? Alas, a quarter pounder is an hors d'oeuvre for a pro gurgitator. Don Lerman set his sights on quarter-pound Cloud burgers, downing just over eleven of 'em in ten minutes. Reigning king of the gurgitators Joey Chestnut gobbled 103 Krystal burgers in a mere eight minutes, while Bob Shoudt managed thirty-nine of the Krystal burgers in just two minutes. Sonya Thomas took on three-quarter-pound Thick-burgers, of which she ate seven in ten minutes, and in 2006 managed to snarf down more than eight pounds of Der Wiener-schnitzel chili cheese fries in ten minutes. Geez, it takes longer than that to negotiate their drive-thru window. Not to be outdone, Cookie Jarvis pounded almost four and a half pounds of crinkle-cut fries from Nathan's in six minutes, and also set the record for Pomme Frites, eating two pounds nine ounces in eight minutes. And then there's the nine-pound Big Daddy cheese-burger that Thomas gobbled down in twenty-seven minutes at the Plaza Hotel Casino in 2006. Nine pounds. Think about it. . . .

Baseball Boneheads

In a brave confession before a grand jury in late 2004, major league home run record holder Barry Bonds admitted to using performance enhancing substances—sort of. Bonds claimed he was told that the suspicious "clear" substance and "cream" were given to him by personal trainer and BALCO disgrace Greg Anderson during the 2003 season, and that they were simply nutritional flaxseed oil and balm for arthritis. Steroids? Heavens no! The cream turned out to be the human growth hormone Depo-Testosterone, and the clear stuff was an infertility drug designed to mask the presence of steroids. Busted! Bonds was apparently unaware that other players used exactly the same substances obtained from Anderson, and what was worse, they knew exactly what they were and were happily telling investigators everything to avoid prosecution. So did Anderson purposely keep good 'ol Barry in the dark by secretly slipping illegal drugs to the man who would smash Hank Aaron's 775 career home run record? Not bloody likely. Bonds was indicted for perjury on November 15, 2007. And his record-breaking homer? That'll be remembered with a big fat *asterisk next to it.
*Cheater.

The Dumb Jock Dictionary

Sports terms and what dimwit sportsers think they are!

Balk: *The sound a chicken makes*

Scoreboard: *A little black book*

World Cup: *An international testicle protector*

Oddball Athletics

A strange cross between volleyball and soccer, *sepak takraw* is a wild Indonesian game where three opposing players attempt to smash a rock-hard rattan ball back and forth over a net using only their feet, knees, shoulders, and of course, their heads. Front flips, back flips, and crazy gymnastics come into frenzied play, with headaches being the common denominator. It's like playing soccer with a piece of granite. Can you say Excedrin?

Football Faux Pas

Bruce Walker was a defensive lineman for the New England Patriots in 1996 when he was stabbed in the chest in North Attleboro, Massachusetts. Was he viciously attacked by some thugs? Nope. He and a buddy were throwing a steak knife at each other in the parking lot of a grocery store and Walker missed the catch. He required several stitches and was treated at a local hospital. The six-foot-four, 310-pound giant told *The Sun Chronicle* that he was "puzzled by the interest in the incident," saying that "nothing happened." Perhaps the interest comes from the stupidity of the situation. Seriously. Who plays catch with steak knives?

Nothing but Net!

Tonya Harding:
www.kneecappersofamerica.org

Pacman Jones:
www.whathappensinvegas.com

Tommy Lasorda:
www.bleepbleepbleep.org

Stupid Says . . .

"I'd like to play for an Italian club, like Barcelona."
—Former English footballer
Mark Draper

I DIDN'T TAKE TESTOSTERONE.
I'M JUST MANLY.
Dennis Mitchell

IF YOU'RE A BOOKIE, CALL MY WIFE.
Wayne Gretzky

Food for Thought

Beans, beans the magical fruit. The more
you eat, the more you ... uh ... bloat.
Apparently that old adage doesn't apply to
pro gurgitators, several of whom take on the
challenge of consuming what many folks
consider taboo for obvious digestive reasons.
Case in point, Don Lerman, who in an
astonishing one minute and forty-eight seconds consumed six pounds of baked beans.
(Take a moment to consider the ramifica-
tions.) Not to be outdone, Dale Boone posted
an equally impressive time of one minute
fifty-two seconds for gulping down eighty-
four ounces of pork and beans. Then there's
wee little Sonya Thomas, who in 2004 consumed almost eight and a half pounds of
long course baked beans, gulping them
down in two minutes and forty-seven seconds. There's no polite way to suggest this,
but after those quantities of beans, consumed in a short period, how could one *not*
become a gassy blowbag the size of Jupiter?
If ever there was a great argument for spon-
taneous combustion, now is the time.

Fan Foolishness

During a 2002 football game between the
Philadelphia Eagles and the Washington
Redskins, police were called in when a fan
fight broke out in the stands. When the cops
were forced to use pepper spray, the cooling
fans on the field caused the spray to drift
behind the Eagle's bench, forcing the players
onto the field with many of the athletes
choking, gagging, and vomiting. The incident took place in the fourth quarter and
caused the game to stop for eight minutes.
Eagles quarterback Donovan McNabb knew
something was up. "Whenever you see your
teammates coming out on the field and
pretty much grabbing their throats or covering their noses, it's a pretty tough situation."
Philadelphia head coach Andy Reid noted
that Eagles linebacker Ike Reese was the
first man down. "He started barfing, and we
all just followed right along. We just walked
onto the field, and I just told them to keep
going."

World Record Wackos

Some people, like Ashrita Furman, were born for Guinness greatness, but not in a traditional way. Furman holds a multitude of athletically endeavored world records including playing 434 hopscotch games in twenty-four hours, 130,000 jump ropes in twenty-four hours, 738 underwater jump ropes in sixty minutes, and a 10k sack race which he accomplished in just over an hour and twenty-five minutes. Not wacko enough? How about walking for twenty-three hours and thirty-five minutes while balancing a milk bottle on his head for a total of almost eight-one miles? Or better yet, Furman jumped close to twenty-four miles in twelve hours and twenty-seven minutes along a college track in New York in 1997. His instrument of choice? A pogo stick.

Stupid Says . . .

66What other problems do you have besides being unemployed, a moron, and a dork?99
—John McEnroe to a tennis spectator

Running on Empty

It's no secret that guys holding the title "World's Fastest Man" have traditionally been known to have egos the size of zeppelins. For Tim Montgomery, you can add übermoron to that title. In the 2000 Sydney Olympics, Montgomery garnered a gold as part of the 4x100 relay team. Two years later, on September 14, he broke the rarely approached world record for 100 meters with a scathing time of 9.78. Being Marion Jones's training partner and future baby daddy, and having Trevor Graham as his coach shoulda been the first clue. Despite never testing positive, Montgomery became deeply entrenched in the BALCO steroid scandal and retired before receiving a two-year ban. But that disgrace wasn't enough for Montgomery. In April 2006, he was arrested for his involvement in a $5 million bank fraud and money laundering scheme that included altered, stolen, or counterfeit checks—a scheme that dragged Jones into the mix when she deposited one of those checks. He faces up to four years in the slammer. Could these world-class idiots be any dumber?

WHAT WERE THE WORST EIGHT YEARS IN DENNIS RODMAN'S LIFE?

THE FOURTH GRADE.

Olympic Oops!

This may be hard to believe, but doping cheats at the 2000 Sydney Olympics were actually outdone in regard to unspeakably shameful behavior by members of the Spanish basketball team that took first place in the Paralympics that followed the Games. The Spaniards produced documentation that ten of their team members had intelligence quotients less than eighty-five, which qualified them as intellectually handicapped, but the only mental handicap proved to belong to Spanish authorities who filled the squad with talented ringers who could probably play ball in the NBA. How the subterfuge was exposed is a classic tale of investigative journalism—literally. One of Spain's handicapped hoopsters turned out to be a Spanish reporter who slipped onto the basketball squad after performing six sit-ups and having his blood pressure checked. Zero psychological examination. After the story broke, the disgraced Spaniards were thankfully stripped of their gold medals. In case you're wondering, many national Paralympic basketball teams only require proof that players suffer from ADD or dyslexia for eligibility. Hell, that describes half the players in the NBA.

Moronic Marketing

The top ten products or organizations
moronic jocks should never endorse.

1. Don King: Dippity Doo
2. Michael Vick: The Humane Society
3. Tonya Harding: Trailer Parks of
   America
4. Charles Barkley: Woman's suffrage
5. Dennis Rodman: The National Association of Wedding Planners
6. Marion Jones: All Free and Clear
   detergent
7. Mike Tyson: The Board of Reconstruc-
   tive Surgery
8. Floyd Landis: Huffy Bicycles
9. Darryl Strawberry: The Bureau of Alcohol, Tobacco, and Firearms
10. O.J. Simpson: Rolex, Henckel Knives,
    Ford Broncos, or Tropicana

Stupid Says . . .

66From the waist down, Earl Campbell has the biggest legs I've ever seen on a running back.99

—John Madden

World Record Wackos

You know how you spend hours, days, and weeks at the gym trying to increase your strength in a vain attempt to brag to everyone how much you can bench press? Well, it's time to give up, because Irishman Eamonn Keane has all of us beat by a mile. In July of 2003, Keane went to the World Gym at California's Marina Del Rey and in the course of one hour managed to bench press a total of 305,300 pounds. The world record achievement included 493 repetitions with 100-pound weights and a vein-busting 1,280 reps with 200-pound weights. As you can see, it's perfectly futile that any of us attempt bench pressing. Keane lifted enough for everyone. Pass the Ben Gay. . . .

The Dumb Jock Dictionary

Sports terms and what dimwit sportsers think they are!

Broad jump: *What Wilt Chamberlain claimed to do three times a day*

Quarterback sack: *Joe Namath's playground for nubile actresses*

Unforced error: *Forgetting to wear a condom*

Bumper Snickers!

YES, I DID USE A BOWL TO CUT MY HAIR.
Pete Rose

IF YOU CAN READ THIS: KISS MY ASS. LITERALLY.
Vince McMahon

Scatterbrained Sportsters

Of all the female athletes to make splashes look like belly flops on the American sports scene, Tonya Harding hands down ranks as the trailer-trashiest, and the Nancy Kerrigan debacle was just the tip of the stupidity iceberg. Aside from pathetic forays into pro wrestling and boxing, where she sucked and the fans hated her, she's pulled such idiotic publicity stunts as claiming she was being stalked by professional golfers driving a Lincoln Town Car. Professional golfers? In other bits of Hardingesque absurdity, the fallen ice wench claimed she was abducted by a knife-wielding maniac from whose clutches she barely escaped with her life. Of course, this happened the opening weekend of the 1997 U.S. Figure Skating Championships. Coincidence? Not bloody likely. In 2007, Harding once again irritated cops, claiming armed intruders were creeping around her Florida property trying to steal her car and hide their firearms. Once again, police determined that the Hall of Shamer has an overactive imagination. One thing's for certain: she *still* sucks and fans *still* hate her.

Mix and Mingle:
Asinine Athlete Anagrams

1. Surya Bonaly
2. Tim Hardaway
3. Wade Boggs
4. Johann Mulegg
5. Ilie Nastase
6. Lloyd Eisler
7. Mary Decker
8. O.J. Simpson
9. Tommy Lasorda
10. Michael Vick

a. EYELIDS ROLL
b. RACK REMEDY
c. EASIEST NAIL
d. MOPS JOINS
e. MALADY MOTORS
f. DRAMA HAYWIT
g. HACK LICE VIM
h. BAGGED SOW
i. MAHJONG HE LUNG
j. SNARLY BAYOU

*Answers: 1-j,
2-f, 3-h, 4-i,
5-c, 6-a, 7-b,
8-d, 9-e, 10-g*

Jailbird Jocks

Too many sports stars seem to head straight into the black hole of self destruction, which is the unfortunate legacy of prodigious slugger Darryl Strawberry, who helped the Mets and the Yankees into four World Series and was voted to the All-Star Game eight consecutive times during his major league career. Strawberry hit the majors in 1983, but by 1987 he started hitting the skids with growing substance abuse problems and accusations and arrests for domestic violence. Strawberry's first wife, Lisa, accused the slugger of breaking her nose in 1987, and again in 1990 when he slapped her and pulled a pistol during a stoned rage. Divorced in 1993, he was also arrested for beating his pregnant girlfriend. Scattered into the mix were more arrests and league suspensions for drug use, and by 2000 his brushes with the law became serious. By March of 2002, Strawberry was tossed in the pokey for eleven months after violating earlier drug related probations, which was the last straw toward effectively killing his career. For the once-great slugger, fame and success turned into a seriously sticky Strawberry jam.

Basketball Buffoons

At six-foot-seven, the heavily inked, pierced,
and multicolor-coiffed Dennis Rodman is an
NBA enigma. During his tenure with the
Chicago Bulls, Rodman was known for wild
behavior, once head-butting referee Ted
Bernhardt—whose decisions he disagreed
with—during a game against New Jersey.
In another famous incident, he kicked a television cameraman in the tender parts after
tripping over the poor guy. That little temper
tantrum cost Rodman $200,000 in an out-of-
court settlement. Off-court, Rodman is
equally unpredictable, often exhibiting his
penchant for wearing lipstick and eye
shadow and once showing up at a book promotion in a wedding dress. In 1997, Rodman
skipped practices with the Bulls to venture
into pro wrestling, where he teamed up with
Hulk Hogan to take on the tag team of Lex
Luger and The Giant. And just to round out
the horror, the tattooed wonder made an
infamously horrible attempt at acting with
Jean-Claude Van Damme in the 1997 flick
Double Team. For his efforts, Rodman
earned three Razzies as Worst New Star,
Worst Supporting Actor, and Worst Screen
couple with Van Damme. Musta been the
wedding dress.

The Oddball Sport of the Millennium Award

Got a nagging wife? Love sports? Boy have we got a sport for you. What better way to shut your mate's yap than entering the Wife-Carrying World Championship, which involves men carrying a female on their back over a 253.5 meter track containing gravel, sand, and grass, and two dry and one water obstacles. Originated in Sonkajärvi, Finland, the race pays homage to legendary Finnish brigand, Rosvo-Ronkainen, who made potential gang members run through the forest carrying hefty sacks on their backs. Carrying strategies for the race include piggyback style, over the shoulder, or hanging the wife upside down with her legs flung over her he-man's shoulders. According to the rules, the "wife" can be any woman of your choosing as long as she's over seventeen and at least 107 pounds. At the 2007 Championship, forty-four couples from twelve different countries competed. Estonians took the gold and silver medals with Madis Uusorg and partner Inga Klauson finishing first in 61.7 seconds. What was the grand prize? A plasma TV for each and Klauson's weight in beer. Bottoms up!

Bumper Snickers!

I'M NOT PROMISCUOUS. I'M JUST VIRILE!
Wilt Chamberlain

CAUTION: FAUX GOLD MEDAL
WINNER ONBOARD.
Paul Hamm

The Dumb Jock Dictionary

Sports terms and what dimwit sportsers
think they are!

Doping: *One of the seven dwarves*

Bump and run: *A one-night stand*

Sudden death: *What happens when
you're a WWE wrestler*

Oddball Athletics

Most of us have heard of the repulsive Scottish delicacy known as haggis, which is comprised of sheep entrails stuffed into a sheep's stomach and boiled for hours. But the Scots have taken the concoction to new lows with a competition called "haggis hurling," where opponents stand atop a whiskey barrel and fling a haggis for distance. If you've ever tasted the stuff, you've probably figured out a much different way to hurl it.

Nothing but Net!

Charles Barkley:
www.imachauvinistpig.com

Amy Van Dyken:
www.igotmyasskicked.org

Trevor Graham:
www.whistleblower.com

Food for Thought

Since childhood it has been engrained in all of us that fruits and vegetables are good for us. Competitive eaters have taken that concept to the extreme. For starters, there's Joey Chestnut, who at the 2007 Stockton Asparagus Fest gobbled up just over eight and a half pounds of tempura deep-fried asparagus spears in a mere ten minutes. Cookie Jarvis showed equal fervor in 2005 when he made short work of almost nine pounds of grapes, eating them in ten minutes. Then there's Charles Hardy who, living up to his name, went to battle with a gianormous six-pound-nine-ounce cabbage. The poor little thing didn't stand a chance—Hardy devoured it in nine minutes. The same went for 2.71 pounds of French-cut green beans, which were consumed in six minutes by Crazy Legs Conti. Not to be outdone was Eric Booker, who downed nine and a half one-pound bowls of peas in twelve minutes. In 2004, Booker also polished off more than a half pound of Maui onions in one minute. Pass the Altoids. . . .

Scatterbrained Sportsters

It's fair to say that if you're a world champion boxer, the last thing in the world you should be doing is dressing up in black heels and a fishnet bodysuit and letting some wily stripper snap your picture. Apparently Oscar de la Hoya didn't get *that* memo. Idiot! As the "Golden Boy" of the 1992 Barcelona Olympics, the former super welterweight phenom managed to turn himself into an industry, and made himself a very rich man in the process. But 2007 wasn't a good year for 'ol Oscar, as he got slapped with a $100 million lawsuit filed by Milana Dravnel, a twenty-two-year-old ex-stripper with whom he allegedly had a year-long affair. Apparently, Oscar has a thing for women's lacy underthings and allowed her to snap the pics, which she sold for $70,000, and which appreared on the Internet. Oops. Of course, Oscar denied their authenticity, and for that, the lusty Siberian Dravnel is suing him, claiming the smear campaign against her— not to mention fraud, defamation, emotional distress, and other sordid charges—are worth $100 million. Did we mention that Oscar is hitched and awaiting the arrival of a child?

HOW DO YOU CONFUSE
TONYA HARDING?

YOU DON'T.
SHE WAS BORN THAT WAY.

Who's on First?

For wacky entertainment value, pro wrestling is in an indescribable class of its own, and it probably couldn't maintain its insane popularity without the influence of Vincent Kennedy McMahon, who single-handedly turned the concept of pay-per-view television into a multimillion-dollar industry. Under McMahon's tutelage, pro wrestling went from a trashy parking lot sideshow that featured fat guys hucking folding chairs at each other's heads to a trashy big ticket venue with wildly disparate audiences of toothless hillbillies and yuppies who hide their WWE obsession from colleagues out of sheer embarrassment. One of McMahon's favorite gimmicks is the infamous "Kiss My Ass Club," where wrestlers and WWE members are forced to enter the ring and kiss McMahon's bare buttocks in a public act of humiliation. Lovely. With McMahon's iron grasp over the business and with their jobs on the line, no ass kissers have had the courage to decline the indignity. At the forefront of McMahon's hokey wrestling storylines, the savvy promoter has established himself as the premier "bad guy" in pro wrestling, and it has made him millions. The latter, however, is no reason to kiss the guy's hiney.

World Record Wackos

Water sport lovers take note of the following
nutty world records—they're a pair of
doozies. On a good day it takes a fair amount
of strength and coordination to handle a jet
ski. On a bad day, you just end up in the
drink. But that wasn't the case for Croatian
Davor Hundic who took on a daunting distance record for an aquabike. In June of
2005, riding an RX Sea-Doo, Hundic drove
for twenty-four hours straight and covered a
whopping 600 miles. If that doesn't wet your
whistle, then consider the record for water
slide riding, set in Bremen, Germany, in
November 2005. In the span of twenty-four
hours, the equivalent of over 472 miles was
covered by a group of ten employees. The
number of wedgies received by said sliders
remains unknown and, no doubt,
irreparable.

Stupid Says . . .

66Boxing is the only sport you can get your brain shook, your money took, and your name in the undertaker book.99
—Joe Frazier

Extreme Sports from Hell

Top ten sports that should *never* be included in the Olympic Games:

1. Female tapioca wrestling
2. Sloth tossing
3. Arctic ice fishing
4. 100-meter beer bonging
5. Fabergé egg tossing
6. Midget sumo bowling
7. Jell-o diving
8. Monster truck tire discus throwing
9. Tidal wave belly boarding
10. Naked ski jumping

Olympic Oops!

The infamous Iron Curtain hid more than the misery of millions of East Germans. It also hid a State run program to dope athletes with steroids in a rampant organized drug abuse scheme. In 1972, East German athletes took home twenty gold medals at the Munich Olympics, but that number doubled in just four years at Montreal's 1976 Games. Then they repeated the astonishingly unlikely—and suspicious—feat at the 1980 Moscow Games. In 2000, East Germany's sports chief, Manfred Ewald, and medical director, Dr. Manfred Hoeppner, admitted to doping more than 140 young female athletes without their knowledge in a cheating scandal that caused irreparable harm to the Olympics, East Germany's reputation, and unfortunately the women themselves, who still suffer the effects of steroid abuse. Shot putter Heidi Krieger was even forced to undergo a sex change operation because her body was so severely altered by male hormones. Ewald and Hoeppner received relatively minor fines and were given probation. Instead of a slap on the wrist, we think those two should've had their own male parts permanently reassigned. Scumbags.

Going Mental

Match the athletic neuroses to its prognosis.

1. Wiltaphobia
2. Vickaphobia
3. Tysonaphobia
4. Barrybondaphobia
5. Rodmanophobia
6. Delahoyaphobia
7. Kerriganophobia
8. Barkleyaphobia
9. Cansecophobia
10. Benoitaphobia

a. Fear of perjury
b. Fear of vindictive ex-strippers
c. Fear of offending Mickey Mouse
d. Fear of snitches
e. Fear of 'roid rage
f. Fear of condoms
g. Fear of feminists
h. Fear of P.E.T.A.
i. Fear of wedding dresses
j. Fear of scary facial tats

Answers: 1-f,
2-h, 3-j, 4-a,
5-i, 6-b, 7-c,
8-g, 9-d, 10-e

WHY DID WILT CHAMBERLAIN NAME HIS MANHOOD?

HE HAD TO BE ON A FIRST NAME BASIS WITH THE ONE WHO MADE ALL HIS DECISIONS.

Gold Medal Gaffes

The 2004 Olympic Games in Athens was a brilliantly historic celebration, but dopers weren't the only ones making headlines. A few NBC commentators stepped up to the plate (or stepped in it, as it were) and we can't help but pay homage to these classic blunders.

66This is really a lovely horse and I speak from personal experience since I once mounted her mother.99

—Horse racing commentator Ted Walsh

66This is Gregoriava from Bulgaria. I saw her snatch this morning during her warm up and it was amazing.99

—Weightlifting commentator at the Snatch and Jerk Event

66Ah, isn't that nice, the wife of the IOC president is hugging the cox of the British crew.99

—Commentator at a rowing medal ceremony

66One of the reasons Andy is playing so well is that, before the final round, his wife takes out his balls and kisses them. . . . Oh my God, what have I just said?99

—Tennis commentator

66Julian Dicks is everywhere. It's like they've got eleven Dicks on the field.99

—Soccer commentator

Oddball Athletics

If you want to impress your guests at your next cocktail party, ask them if they're familiar with a competition called "sport stacking." It's likely no one will have a clue, so you can explain that it involves stacking plastic cups on top of each other in predetermined sequences to see how high you can get them before they topple. Seriously. There are even tournaments put on by the World Sport Stacking Association, which changed the name from "cup stacking" to "sport stacking" to give it credibility as a "real" sport. Do you suppose the champs are whistling Dixie?

The Dumb Jock Dictionary

Sports terms and what dimwit sportsers think they are!

Lob: *Where you get your ears pierced*

Starting gun: *Your first Beretta*

Infield fly: *Struggling with a sticky zipper*

Bumper Snickers!

A FOOL AND HIS MONEY ARE
A MISTRESS' BEST FRIEND.
Oscar de la Hoya

FISH TREMBLE AT THE SOUND
OF MY NAME.
Amy Van Dyken

Stupid Says . . .

"It's not that I dislike many people. It's just that I don't like many people.**"**
—Bryant Gumbel

Food for Thought

What do you usually eat for breakfast? Toast and coffee? An omelet? Perhaps a cinnamon roll? For a normal eater that's a sensible meal, but for a pro gurgitator, that's a tidbit. Case in point: Crazy Legs Conti, who wiped out three and a half pounds of bacon and pancakes in twelve minutes. That's less time than it takes most of us to prepare them. The same goes for huevos rancheros, a dish which, believe it or not, has its own world record. In 2006, Richard LeFevre downed seven and three quarter pounds of huevos in ten minutes flat. To further expand the horror of competitive breakfast food, one must also pay homage to Patrick Bertoletti, who in September 2007 required only ten minutes to polish off twenty-one pounds of grits. Eek! But it doesn't stop there. In 2007, he downed twenty-nine waffles in ten minutes, and also owns the record for glazed and cream-filled donuts, having chowed down forty-seven of 'em in a mere five minutes. Also on the donut wagon is Eric Booker, who annihilated forty-nine glazed confections in eight minutes. Death by Krispy Kreme. It's only a matter of time. . . .

Running on Empty

Some athletes who should be revered for their greatness are sometimes reviled as a result of controversy. Such is the case with America's greatest distance runner, Mary Decker Slaney. At the top of her game for years, Slaney was the heavy favorite for gold at the 1984 Los Angeles Olympics. On August 11, the stage was set for the 3,000 meters, a race featuring Slaney and eighteen-year-old South African phenom Zola Budd. With expedited British citizenship, Budd was a slight ninety-two pound wonder who actually raced barefoot. Early in the race, Budd and Decker bumped elbows, but around 1,600 meters, disaster struck. As Budd moved to pass Decker, Budd's foot touched her leg. With four runners bunched up, the two women lost stride. Decker's foot hit Budd's calf and Budd went off balance. Decker grabbed the number off the back of Budd's shirt and then went headfirst into the infield. The American crowd went insane, completely unnerving Budd, who finished seventh. Refusing to accept Budd's apology, Slaney began a bitter campaign to publicly blame her for the accidental collision. In 1996, Slaney began a long legal battle after failing a urine test. Sour grapes anyone?

Imbecilic Cretin of the Millennium Award

On November 28, 2007, pathological narcissist O.J. Simpson pleaded not guilty along with two codefendants to charges stemming from the robbery of sports memorabilia dealers Bruce Fromong and Alfred Beardsley. The dealers were in a Vegas hotel room September 13 with another dealer named Thomas Riccio when an enraged O.J. arrived with a pair of armed companions. A terminal sleaze bucket, Riccio is alternately credited or accused of setting up the encounter, having tipped off Juice to the whereabouts of stolen memorabilia. Riccio recorded much of the confrontation, which was notoriously leaked to the media. The three alleged outlaws will be in court in March 2008 to face a cocktail of offenses including kidnapping, armed robbery, assault with a deadly weapon, burglary, coercion, and conspiracy, which could land them in the slammer for the rest of their lives. Simpson claims to have simply been recovering stolen property with the help of his buddies. Uh huh. By the end of 2007, Simpson's pals accepted plea bargains in return for implicating him. If the Juice is a twit, you *can't* acquit. . . .

WHAT DO HOCKEY
FANS CONSIDER A
SEVEN COURSE MEAL?

A HOT DOG
AND A SIX PACK.

Baseball Boneheads

While steroid abuse is a major threat to the integrity of professional baseball, there are instances where outright cheating reaches all the way down to the Little Leagues. The most dominant pitcher in the 2001 Little League World Series was a kid named Danny Almonte, whose father flew with him to New York from their home in the Dominican Republic to participate in the event as the star pitcher for the Bronx league's All Stars. Almonte pitched a perfect game in the series, mowing down batters one after the other. Fortunately, league rules prevent the same pitcher from playing every game, but still, the Bronx team finished third. Not too shabby for a competition that features the best players from around the world. But there was one . . . uh . . . minor problem. Almonte was actually fourteen—two years older than the mandatory age limit of twelve. Oops. His father was charged in the Dominican Republic for faking his son's birth certificate and the Bronx team forfeited all of their wins. For some people, Little League is less a field of dreams than it is a field of schemes.

Oddball Athletics

You've heard of skateboarding and snow-
boarding, right? If so, it should come as no
surprise that some ignoramus came up with
the grand idea of combining the two by
developing an oversized skateboard with
large rubber wheels made for careening
down mountain slopes. Mountainboarding is
the ideal way edgy snowboarders can hone
their skills during the off-season—and break
a few bones in the process. Hang ten, dude!

World Record Wackos

Under the heading of "some people are
insane," meet Pakistani Zafar Gill, who in
2004 attached a clamp to his right ear and
lifted more than 113 pounds of gym weights.
He held them for seven seconds. No doubt
you're clutching your earlobes as we speak. . . .

The Dumb Jock Dictionary

Sports terms and what dimwit sportsers think they are!

Full-court press: *The media at Michael Vick's trial*

Buzzer beater: *A bottle of aspirin after a night at the sport's bar*

Line judge: *A coke dealer*

Bumper Snickers!

I BRAKE FOR STEROIDS!
Ben Johnson

I GOT AWAY WITH IT. YOU CAN TOO!
Mark McGwire

Football Faux Pas

There's a touchy subject that has befuddled and bemused football fans—and especially the frazzled wives and girlfriends of gridiron nuts. What the hell's up with the butt slapping? You often see players smash into each other chest first in gleeful acts of triumph and celebration, but when the chips are down and it's time to go out there and win one for the Gipper, things get ugly. Grown men slap each other on the fanny like the flanks of a prize bull. Boys learn the fanny-smack as little gridiron crawlers in the Pop Warner League, continue it through high school, and even spin Grandpa's *corpus delecti* in the funeral home just to give the old guy a farewell slap on the caboose. Is it a compliment? A simple "Atta boy!?" Is it cuz footballers are so heavily armored there's no place on their bodies they can feel a slap? It's one of the great mysteries of life. Do it to your wife, she'll think you're looking for a little action. Do it to a lap dancer, you'd better have a ten-spot in your hand. Do it to a 300-pound linebacker you'd better be damn sure you're well padded.

Food for Thought

Why did the chicken cross the road? To escape the competitive eater. And for good reason. Pro gurgitators have a field day with fowl and they make no bones about it. Top eater Joey Chestnut is no slouch in the poultry department, owning a trio of impressive records. It took him only thirty minutes to devour 182 long-form chicken wings, and a mere twelve minutes in 2007 to destroy seven and a half pounds of buffalo wings. In 2006, during Nisea Week, Chestnut downed 212 chicken and vegetable gyoza in ten minutes. For Sonya Thomas, chicken nuggets proved to be equally record breaking, as the waifish wonder plowed through eighty in a mind-bending five minutes. And adding two more record cluckers to the list is Cookie Jarvis, who offed just over two pounds of short-form chicken wings from Hooters in a quick five minutes, and six eleven-ounce chicken fried steaks in twelve minutes. And yes, the steaks included gravy. There is no end to the madness that is competitive eating.

Scatterbrained Sportsters

For a country like Bulgaria, it's devastating when one of their national heroes takes a dive. Maxim Staviski and his partner Albena Denkova are a stunning couple in the insanely competitive world of ice dancing. As 2006 and 2007 world champions, they were finally at the top of their game. But that changed in the blink of an eye. On August 5, 2007, Staviski was driving though a Black Sea town in Bulgaria when he swerved his SUV in the oncoming lane resulting in a head-on collision that killed twenty-four-year-old Petar Petrov and left Petrov's eighteen-year-old female companion in a coma. It's alleged the Russian-born Staviski's blood test showed twice the legal alcohol limit. To his credit, a devastated Staviski said he was "Ready to take any punishment," which in this case could be spending anywhere from three to ten years in prison. Sadly, it's unlikely that anyone in the pen will appreciate his rumba.

The Dumb Jock Dictionary

Sports terms and what dimwit sportsers think they are!

Two-minute warning: *The motel manager banging on the door to tell you that your hour's up*

Double dribble: *Having a few too many and drooling over your jersey*

Broadsiding: *What got Kobe Bryant in trouble*

Oddball Athletics

The sport of moving efficiently and quickly over obstacles such as tree branches, fences, walls, rocks, or whatever might be in your path in an emergency situation has a name: *le art du déplacement*. Popularly known as *parkour*, or the art of displacement, there's really nothing else like it in the sports world, with participants traveling over whatever predetermined courses or obstacles strike their fancy whether it's climbing trees, bounding over rocks, or scaling walls with incredible speed and efficiency. It's like Cirque du Soleil meets *Crouching Tiger, Hidden Dragon*, only without the fancy clothes and swords. Most definitely not a sport for couch potatoes.

HOW WILL
O.J. SIMPSON'S
BRAIN CELLS DIE?

A L O N E .

Baseball Boneheads

One of the most infamous capers in minor league history happened on a warm August night in 1987 during a game in Williamsport, Pennsylvania, between the Williamsport Bills and the Reading Phillies. It was late in the season and both teams were so far out of the pennant race that simply showing up for the nearly pointless showdown was a tedious chore for the players. In an effort to liven up the proceedings, catcher Dave Bresnahan, an eighteenth-round draft pick for the Cleveland Indians who was playing catcher for their Williamsport farm team, made plans to swap a hand carved potato for the game ball. After catching a well-timed pitch late in the fifth inning, Bresnahan surreptitiously swapped the ball for the spud and rifled it over the third baseman's head into left field. Thinking he had a free ride, the runner jogged toward home plate where Bresnahan tagged him out with the real baseball. Funny? Hell yes, although the fuming umpire gave the score to the runner, and the humorless Bills manager fined Bresnahan fifty bucks and cut him from the roster the next day. Mr. Potato Head is still laughing his nose off.

Basketball Buffoons

Professional basketball players aren't necessarily known for rational thought, but when it comes to out-and-out male chauvinism, Charles Barkley takes the cake. In a 2002 interview with *Stuff* magazine, Barkley made it clear that he doesn't think women should be involved in sports—any sport. Nor does the idiot think women should be in the army—any army. Where does he think women should be? "On *Temptation Island*. Naked. With me." Lovely. And when it comes to his fans he's just as condescending, saying that he hates regular people who voice their opinions about sports because they're just fans. If you happen to be a Barkley fan, get over it. He doesn't need fans. He needs ten minutes in a locked room with Gloria Steinem. Preferably with Steinem holding a Taser.

Nothing but Net!

Stone Cold Steve Austin:
www.ibeatupoldladies.com

Oscar de la Hoya:
www.ilovefishnets.com

Mike Nifong:
www.vendettagonewrong.org

The Dumb Jock Dictionary

Sports terms and what dimwit sportsers think they are!

Mixed doubles: *Cosmos and mojitos*

Handicap: *What Don King needs to cover his head*

Olympiad: *A beer commercial*

Food for Thought

When it comes to sandwiches, competitive eaters are out of control. In addition to being the pulled pork sandwich champ, Joey Chestnut holds the record for grilled cheese sandwiches (forty-seven in ten minutes) and Horseshoe sandwiches (almost six and a half pounds in twelve minutes). Following on Chestnut's heels is up and comer Chip Simpson, who set a new record at the New York State Fair in 2006, when he demolished more than thirteen Gianelli sausage sandwiches in twelve minutes. But like Chestnut, high-ranking champ Patrick Bertoletti is holding his own in the sandwich realm. The current corned beef sandwich champ, Bertoletti also set the record for date nut bread and cream cheese sandwiches, eating nearly thirty of 'em in eight minutes. Even more amazing is his peanut butter and jelly sandwich record. Accomplished in 2007, Bertoletti somehow managed to slough down forty-two of the sticky snackers in ten minutes. It boggles the mind.

Who's on First?

One of the greatest baseball players of all time will probably never by inducted into the Hall of Fame, and it's entirely his own fault. In May of 1989, Major League investigators turned up damning documentation that Cincinnati Reds manager Pete Rose placed bets on fifty-two Reds games at a minimum of $10,000 per game. To his credit, none of the bets were ever placed against the Reds, but gambling in any form is a huge no-no for big leaguers. Rose steadfastly denied any involvement in betting on any team, but the evidence said otherwise. He was relieved of his managing duties and made ineligible for major league activity and, in 1991, the Hall of Fame voted to exclude anyone on the ineligible list from being inducted—a solid slap in the face to Rose who was a Hall of Fame shoo-in. In 2004, Rose finally confessed his gambling habit in his autobiography, *My Prison Without Bars*, destroying any chance of ever joining the most prestigious club in major league sports. It's possible a future change in major league attitudes could alter his standing—just don't bet on it.

Nothing but Net!

Tim Montgomery:
www.worldsfastestcriminal.com

Tom Brady:
www.imdoingasupermodel.org

Vince McMahon:
www.kissmyhiney.com

The Dumb Jock Dictionary

Sports terms and what dimwit sportsers think they are!

Hole-in-one: *What O.J. has in his head*

Formula One: *What your baby mama needs*

Archery: *A foot fetish*

Oddball Athletics

Some sports should never have been invented on grounds of sheer lunacy and brutality. Sheep tackling, a popular half-time entertainment during New Zealand rugby matches, drew inevitable cries of brutality from animal rights groups—particularly because there were kids involved. The hilarious concept involved dressing sheep in rugby shirts and letting the kiddies loose on them in teams of five in an effort to wrestle the wooly buggers to the ground. The anti-cruelty folks scored the final victory by getting the game banned forever. It must be said. This sport was a *baaaaad* idea.

Moronic Monikers

The five nicknames boneheaded jocks should've had:

1. Oscar "Fishnet" de la Hoya
2. Michael "Rabid Dog" Vick
3. Nancy "Princess Whiny Pants" Kerrigan
4. Marion "Flaxseed" Jones
5. Joe "Super Lech" Namath

Bumper Snickers!

I TOOK AN I.Q. TEST AND THE RESULTS WERE NEGATIVE.
Tim Hardaway

I'M NOT FLIPPING YOU THE BIRD. I'M JUST POINTING AT THE SCENERY.
Bobby Knight

World Record Wackos

If given a choice, chances are most folks wouldn't choose "head balancer" as a lifetime career. Odd as it may sound, that is the athletic profession of Brit John Evans who over the years has balanced an abundance of people, beer, and literature, and broken more than twenty-five different records. But Evans's *pièce de résistance* occurred in 1999, when for thirty-three seconds, he balanced a car on his head. Yes, a car. A 352-pound gutted Mini Cooper to be exact. Ouch. And if that isn't painful enough, check out Frank Simon. In 1999, the Hungarian wonder balanced a motorcycle and helmet on his teeth for fourteen seconds. Total weight? A mindboggling 135 pounds. Hope he has his dentist on speed dial. Oh, and lest we forget, there's Arulanantham Suresh Joachim who holds the record for balancing on one foot, which he achieved in 1997. Joachim managed the "feat" for seventy-six hours and forty minutes. We're betting he's never failed a sobriety test.

Oddball Athletics

No book that delves into athletic lunacy would be complete without mentioning one of the more bizarre sports that most of us have engaged in at one time or another—thumb wresting. Yep. It's still being played. For television watching kiddies there's even the *Thumb Wrestling Federation,* which features costumed thumbs battling it out in the ring. As far as stupid sports go, we still give this one a thumb's up for nostalgia's sake.

Linguistics 101

Legendary Florida State football coach Bill Peterson uttered so many classic statements that we'd be woefully remiss not to include a few gems. With a reputation for being the "Coach of Coaches," Peterson did well to train a host of future NFL coaches. He would, however, have greatly benefited from a syntax coach!

66You guys pair up in groups of three, then line up in a circle.99

66Men, I want you just thinking of one word all season. One word and one word only: Super Bowl.99

66You guys line up alphabetically by height.99

66I'm the football coach around here and don't you remember it.99

66The greatest thing just happened to me. I just got indicted into the Florida Sports Hall of Fame. They had a standing observation for me.99

66I used to have this slight speech implement and couldn't remember things before I took the Sam Carnegie course.99

Mix and Mingle:
Asinine Athlete Anagrams

1. Nancy Kerrigan
2. Lance Armstrong
3. Svetlana Khorkina
4. Justin Gatlin
5. Jesse Ventura
6. Martina Hingis
7. Wilt Chamberlain
8. Kostas Kenteris
9. Oscar de la Hoya
10. Steve Garvey

a. SAGE VERYVET
b. MACABRE HILLTWIN
c. TARNISHING AIM
d. ARCADE LAYSHOO
e. ACME GNARL SNORT
f. RANKLE KNAVISHOAT
g. SNAKIEST STOKER
h. CRANKY GRANNY
i. SLAIN JUTTING
j. SEVERE JAUNTS

Answers: 1-h,
2-e, 3-f, 4-i,
5-j, 6-c, 7-b,
8-g, 9-d, 10-a

219

Bumper Snickers!

CAUTION. SNITCH ONBOARD.
Trevor Graham

ANOTHER DAY. ANOTHER PIÑA COLADA.
Oksana Baiul

Nothing but Net!

Jose Canseco:
www.couldibeanydumber.org

Michael Jordan:
www.mywifetookmetothecleaners.com

Lance Armstrong:
www.ineverdopedup.org

Oddball Athletics

If you're a strictly hands-off athlete who prefers to let technology do all the dirty work, then you'll be in hog heaven playing RoboCup Soccer, a game in which two teams of eleven "virtual agents" guided by computers try to knock a ball into goals. For those who'd like to get more involved, there's even one class of competition that allows personal control with hand-held transmitters. Who says computer geeks can't be jocks?

Stupid Says . . .

"Anybody who watches three games of football in a row should be declared brain dead."

—Erma Bombeck